A LIGHT TO

MY PATH

By

JOSHUA GONZALES

i

DEDICATED

I dedicate this book to Jesus Christ, My Lord and Savior.

The one who bore my sins on the cross and healed me from drugs and took the punishment of my sins upon him and gave me Everlasting life.

I also dedicate this book to my Mother and Father, who fervently prayed for me for over 30 years to return to Christ. Thank you, if it was not for you and God I would not be here.

I also dedicate this book to my son, who has witnessed my transformation. I love you buddy with all of my heart, if you hadn't come into my life I wouldn't have gotten so far. God used you to keep me on track, through you I have also seen God's transforming grace.

I also dedicate this book to all of my friends and the rest of my family; you have also witnessed my transformation in God's Grace.

A big shout to the heavens hosanna, in the highest blessed be your mighty name, may your transforming power be declared throughout the world.

INTRODUCTION

I hope you find this book refreshing and encouraging. I was not always on the path that am on now, for many years I was not following God, and it was not until I was 40 years I became a true follower of Christ. My entire life was a void that needed to be filled. I was born on June 13th, 1979 in Algona Iowa. My birth was rare, I was born with chicken pox. My mother somehow had contracted chicken pox virus. The doctors told my mother it was very rare and a miracle. I did not die in the womb or was born with birth defects, Satan had already had his hands on me, he wanted me to die because he knew God had a purpose and a plan for my life and he tried to stop it since the time I was in the womb. That is how Satan works and tries to stop what God has ordained.

I grew up in Burt, Iowa, a small town of less than 500 people. I can remember my parents were at a person's house who they went to church with. I must have been 4 years old but I still remember what I said, that I went to school in Burt from Kindergarten to 7th grade as a child. I had the fire of God. I was an avid sports fan, I loved football and we kids would love going to the park to play. I was the one that got on the phone and got all of my friends together. This gift that God gave me, still stands today drawing people together.

I grew up going to church three times per week. My parents became born-again Christians in 1982, my mom was instantly transformed, but my dad took a little bit longer than her. I was baptized at 9 years old, my pastor asked me where Jesus lived, and I screamed in my heart, I loved going to church, I was raised in a Pentecostal church, the roots of being that sunk in deep, I loved God and going to church. I have seen many miracles as a boy; demons being cast out, Christians speaking in tongues, and the church operating in signs and wonders the healings that I witnessed were amazing. I was a part of the Thursday Evening Children's Church, a great time. I think I was 9 years old, I went to a children's camp, the theme was Sinbusters based on the movie *'Ghostbusters'*. I can remember this song 'If there is something evil in your neighborhood who are you going to call Sinbusters'. My brother and I sang that song the whole way home back from camp when my parents picked us up, I bet we annoyed them, but I'll never forget that I have a vivid memory.

That was a time in my life when I had the fire of God, however, not too long after that I started to drift away from church, and became less important. I would ask my parents do we have to go. I would make fun of them for praying over a meal in public. My mom got a day job and sometimes she would have to work on the weekends, my brother and I would purposely let my dad sleep in so we wouldn't have to go to church. I got into things I should have not gotten into, spending time with friends was way more important than spending time with God. Sports became my idol, video games were up there, so I had begun to mock God. I was embarrassed for even being associated with the church. Most of my friends listened to secular music and I despised my parents for that my friends would poke fun at me because they wouldn't allow me to listen to music that was not Christian. I lived a sheltered life, my parents would always tell us; never do drugs, never drink, never run away from God that went in one ear and out the other.

We went on a family vacation around Christmas time in 1992, we went to Denver, Colorado. My uncle had become a recently born-again Christian, we went to his church close to Christmas. The title of the message was 'Merry Christmas', shortly before his message he pointed at me, young man came forth to the altar. I was like 'Huh' at first, you got the wrong person, I thought he was pointing at someone else but I knew deep down inside that he was pointing at me. I sat there for a few moments, I was terrified... my mother nudged me to go up and see what he wanted, and I got up and started walking towards the altar. I was mocking God the entire time, 'What is this about,' I was laughing in my spirit because I had totally fallen away from God. I got up to the pulpit.

He started talking, 'Young man you have a special calling in your life. You will lead thousands to the Lord,' and then anoints me with oil in front of his congregation. I was laughing in my spirit the entire time, what are you on preacher, you have the wrong person here... me leading thousands to the lord hahaha... no way, Jose, I am not even following God, I want nothing to do with him, how can you even say this nonsense... that's what I was thinking and to think what his congregation was thinking, him bringing a 12-year-old boy to speak this over his life. I wanted nothing to do with what he said.

I went through middle school and high school, and I didn't even try in school, I still passed but I could have done better, looking back on that I wish I had tried harder. Sports in my teenage years was my God, that is all I cared about. I graduated from Central High in 1998. I did not party while I was in high school, although I drank one time and came home drunk and my mom almost killed me. I lived a sheltered life, did not smoke, and never hung out with people who did drugs. My dad always told me how bad drugs were and to never do them, it's a road that will lead to destruction. He told me about his drug days when he was younger, and I told him I would never do that. I eventually went to college in 1998. I was kinda shy back then because I had lived a sheltered life; I had envied my parents for that.

I played sports in high school, so I was pretty athletic. I didn't get to play much because I always got the short end of the stick growing up. I'm sure people can relate to this but when I went to college, I had seen people smoking. One person asked me if I smoked, and I said heck no and I never will. However, that did not last long, guy at the dorms offered me a cigarette, and two days after the first guy offered me one, I thought I would be cool and smoke it. Little did I know what I was getting myself into, 'I lived a sheltered life why not try this, mom and Dad are not here, I am on my own, I can do what I want.' About a week later, when I came back from class, my roommate in college asked me, 'Do you smoke pot?' I did not even know what that word meant. My dad told me about drugs and to never do them but the terminology that was used, I had no clue. He asked me again, 'Do you smoke pot? Do you want to get high?' He showed me the marijuana. I said, 'What on the earth is that?' It is pot-like, I said, 'It was,' 'It's fun to smoke it.' I sat there for a few moments very uncomfortable because then I knew it was drugs. I said, 'No, I don't think so.'

When I went to college, all hell broke loose, the first week I started smoking. I started drinking and was offered drugs, 'What is going on here?' I drank quite a bit during the first two weeks of school. I was very athletic and here I said I would never smoke or drink. I was doing the very thing my parents warned me not to do. A few weeks passed by, and my roommate asked me, 'Do you want to go to these apartments and have a few beers?' 'Yeah, let's go.'

When I got there, I could smell something funky, I asked my roommate, 'What is that awful smell?' he told me, 'It's weed.' I became very uncomfortable, like I was a few weeks prior, when he offered me marijuana. As the night progressed I was asked by the guy that lived in the apartment, who was in my roommate's automotive class. He asked me, 'Do you want to get high?'

I had never done that before; I was scared because it made me uncomfortable. He told me, 'It's not going to kill you, try it you will like it.' I sat there for a few moments, finally, I said. 'Okay, I will try it.' I could not believe what I was doing, the very thing I said, 'I would never do.' I was doing drugs, the high I got was out of this world. I actually liked it enough that it became a habit. After that night, the drinking got worse.

I was not in college now to get an education; I was there to party. I would not dare tell my parents what I was doing. The smoking cigarettes got worse, to the party life was indeed fun, I skipped class a lot, and came in hungover. I went from that sheltered boy, who was shy and insecure to a party animal. Little did I know, what I started in college would end up being a twenty-two-year habit. My grades started dropping.

That year was a complete blaze; every night was a drinking night and getting stoned night. There was not a day gone by that I was not using marijuana. I thought I was cool, I had to do this to fit in the groups who used drugs. Eventually, when my mom found out that I started smoking, she was hurt, she asked me, 'What are you doing?' I was smoking right in front of her, which hurt her even more. I should not have done that. Eventually, she found out I was smoking marijuana. I told her, 'It's okay, it's not hurting anything.' Little did I know, I was hurting the people that loved me.

Eventually, I dropped out of college, the drugs and alcohol took me down a path that I should have said no to from the beginning. The summer of 1999 was a blaze, I had a good job, but I blew it, because I could not say no to drugs and alcohol. This became a trend for twenty-two years. That summer was fun but it wasn't fun for me. I was young and dumb when I got an OWI in the fall of 1999. Lost my license and lost my car. I was driving a 1990 Camaro, that car got me into a lot of trouble.

By this time, God was far out of my life and I cursed God, 'There is no God! All you people are crazy for praying to a Lord that does not exist.' I did not go to church for a long time, I only went on special occasions like Easter and Christmas. My parents were still regular churchgoers and I didn't want anything to do with God. I lost so many jobs from my drug use in the year 2000. I was introduced to meth, and let me tell you, that drug is from the devil. I like it more than marijuana and I used meth the entire summer, not a day went by I was not using it. I used meth from 2000-2010, nearly ten years on and off. My life could have been better, only if I had listened to my parents. God was actually speaking through them to keep me sheltered.

I had lived in Emmetsburg, Iowa from 1998 to 2000, then moved back to Burt, Iowa, my hometown. Many nights I should have died from a drug overdose. It was God keeping me alive for such a far greater purpose than my drug use. I kicked in this time period; I became a father. I did not know I had a son until he was seven months old, he was born in 2008. I still had a problem he was not my priority; drugs were. I would pawn him off and come back a few days later. I would never use drugs around him, through my son, I had a purpose in life. I had gotten a job and had worked at a fast food restaurant for almost eight years, and that was the longest I had ever kept a job.

Sometimes, while I was using drugs and drinking, I would often think about what the preacher said when I was 12 years old; you have a special calling on your life and anointed me with oil, what was that all about? I thought about that at times my entire life, what did he mean by that, I had fallen away from God since 12 years old. Once had a fire as a child, then I grew cold and never went back. I tried to quit smoking and drinking but I was drawn back into the circle, the enemy had a strong hold on me.

Fast through my son, I started going back to church a few times, after he was born, but I did not want anything to do with God. I ended up getting custody of my son in 2010. Little did I know he saved my life; I kept a job, kept food on the table, but I spent the rest of my money on drugs and booze. I was not a good father, even so, I took care of him. If it had not been for my mother, I would have fallen flat on my face, raising a son single is hard.

Fast forward to 2019, I was attending a church and my parents asked me, 'Do you want to go on a retreat?' I said no, at first, then I said, 'Okay, I will go,' but I was only going to go to please them. I went and it changed my life… it was not the retreat it was all God. I had a radical encounter with the Holy Spirit. I had healed from drugs, booze, and smoking in a matter of seconds. Jesus was my rehab. Ever since then, my life has turned upside down and I know what the preacher was saying when he had prophesied over my life. I knew when I left the retreat what he was talking about, it took me twenty-seven years to finally realize what he said. Some nights, while partying, it came to my mind I had a drug habit that lasted two decades. I wish I had been on the path that I am now, serving the Lord, than the path I took in my youth but we can't dwell in the past we have to march forward and do what God has called us to do. I am forever grateful the Lord healed me from my past and gave me a future and a plan that is to stand up for truth and do my best to keep on the path I am now and lead people to the Lord through my testimony.

Some of the context that I have written in the introductions may seem harsh. I am only standing up for truth and what the Bible preaches and teaches, we cannot compromise and condone sin. In the church, I am praying for them to change. I am sharing this out of love, what I went through to get to where I am now has taught me the meaning of life. We have to have a relationship with Jesus, I wish I would have had this twenty years ago. I hope that my testimony throughout this book will help those who have the same problems as I did, struggling with drug and alcohol addictions, and can find Jesus through this book.

All of what I have gone through has brought me to Jesus, my Lord and Savior. I went to church as a child and knew of God but I did not have a relationship with Jesus until I was 40 years old, when he made himself real to me. I had to make a decision to repent, ask for forgiveness, and invite him to come into my heart, saying that my friend is the only way to heaven. I also hope this book will help the body of Christ to remain steadfast in God's word at all times.

Jesus can heal anything if you give him a chance to come into your life. God is using my past to help people overcome their struggles and addictions from substance abuse. I owe Jesus everything, without him I could have never given up my drug addiction. He took it upon himself on the cross, I am forever grateful for taking me back into his kingdom that's just the kind of God he is. Abounding in love he will always take you back in God will use your past for his glory, if you're struggling with anything he can heal you and make you white as snow. My past is my past, I'm pressing forward doing the work of Jesus and he did not promise a bed full of roses, he does promise us everlasting life for those who accept him. The prodigal son has returned home, and he will always welcome you back, even when you drift away. There is nothing you will do that the Father won't welcome you back from (Proverbs 22:6 KJV). We all have a mission that is up to you to let God reveal your calling to you. I am now home rejoicing with God, doing the work that was ordained from the existence of time.

When the Lord formed the Heavens and Earth we were all with him. He was telling us stories of how we would transpire the nations through him and fulfill our callings. I pray that you will be inspired to return to the Lord if you have drifted away and for anyone who is not a Christian to find Jesus through this book. I hope and pray in Jesus' mighty name, Hosanna, in the highest, he will heal you and help you.

Joshua Joseph Gonzales, Sr.

In the Light of Christ, he reigns forever.

Table of Contents

INTRODUCTION ANGER

When we display anger, it shows people that we have things to work on. I used to be a very angry person, I am working on this and I am getting better with the help of the Holy Spirit. I tend to keep things bottled up and sometimes snap. We cannot do this, anger is a tool of Satan, and he wants us to be angry and show the world how foolish we are. When we lose our temper we are all a work in progress, when anger arises, ask the Holy Spirit to help you. He knows you by name and wants to work on this. Growing up, my dad was a very angry person, it is what he went through as a child. I have been trying my hardest to keep my cool in the past five years. God has helped me so much in this area of my life; I am healing from my childhood; I am praying for the generational curse to be broken in the name of Jesus (Yahweh).

How can we work on our anger to let go of this?

Prayer

'Dear Heavenly Father, I pray for the generational curses to be broken and give people healing in Jesus' name.'

ANGER

Cease from anger, and forsake wrath: fret not thyself in any wise to do evil. **Psalm 37:8**

Be ye angry, and sin not: let not the sun go down upon your wrath. **Ephesians 4:26**

A soft answer turneth away wrath: but grievous words stir up anger. **Proverbs 15:1**

Let all bitterness, and wrath, and anger, and clamor, and evil speaking, be put away from you, with all malice. **Ephesians 4:31**

The discretion of a man deferreth his anger and it is his glory to pass over a transgression. **Proverbs 19:11**

A wrathful man stirreth up strife: but he that is slow to anger appeaseth strife. **Proverbs 15:18**

Be not hasty in thy spirit to be angry: for anger resteth in the bosom of fools. **Ecclesias5tes 7:9**

He that is slow to anger is better than the mighty and he that ruleth his spirit than he that taketh a city. **Proverbs 16:32**

An angry man stirreth up strife, and a furious man aboundeth in transgression. **Proverbs 29:22**

Make no friendship with an angry man and with a furious man thou shalt not go:

Lest thou learn his ways and get a snare to thy soul. **Proverbs 22:24-25**

But I say unto you, That whosoever is angry with his brother without a cause shall be in danger of the judgment: and whosoever shall say to his brother, Raca, shall be in danger of the council: but whosoever shall say, Thou fool, shall be in danger of hell fire. **Matthew 5:22**

But now ye also put off all these; anger, wrath, malice, blasphemy, filthy communication out of your mouth. **Colossians 3:8**

Husbands, love your wives and be not bitter against them. **Colossians 3:19**

And, ye fathers, provoke not your children to wrath: but bring them up in the nurture and admonition of the Lord. **Ephesians 6:4**

God judgeth the righteous, and God is angry with the wicked every day. **Psalm 7:11**

Therefore, the LORD was very angry with Israel, and removed them out of his sight: there was none left but the tribe of Judah only. **2 Kings 17:18**

INTRODUCTION ABUNDANCE

God gives us things in abundance when we fully commit to him. I have more than I ever need now. In the first part of my life, I did not have very much because I was not following God. I was chasing worldly desires of the flesh. Once I gave my life back to him my finances tripled, and I got a raise every year from my job. I am so thankful for that, it's a blessing some people do not get a raise like that. God has blessed me supernaturally because I put him first. Your abundance could be manifested more if we fully commit to the lord more.

How can we commit to the Lord more for greater abundance?

Prayer

'Heavenly Father work on us to be more committed to You and show us what it means to fully surrender to Your will.'

ABUNDANCE

For unto every one that hath shall be given, and he shall have abundance: but from him that hath not shall be taken away even that which he hath. **Matthew 5:29**

he thief cometh not, but for to steal, and to kill, and to destroy: I come that they might have life and that they might have it more abundantly. **John 10:10**

Give, and it shall be given unto you; good measure, pressed down, and shaken together, and running over, shall men give into your bosom. For with the same measure that ye mete withal it shall be measured to you again. **Luke 6:38**

The LORD shall open unto thee his good treasure, the heaven to give the rain unto thy land in his season, and to bless all the work of thine hand: and thou shalt lend unto many nations, and thou shalt not borrow. **Deuteronomy 28:12**

Now unto him that is able to do exceeding abundantly above all that we ask or think, according to the power that worketh in us. **Ephesians 3:20**

And the LORD passed by before him, and proclaimed, The LORD, The LORD God, merciful and gracious, longsuffering, and abundant in goodness and truth. **Exodus 34:6**

So shall thy barns be filled with plenty, and thy presses shall burst out with new wine. **Proverbs 3:10**

Thou preparest a table before me in the presence of mine enemies: thou anointest my head with oil; my cup runneth over. **Psalm 23:5**

They shall be abundantly satisfied with the fatness of thy house and thou shalt make them drink of the river of thy pleasures. **Psalm 36:8**

Thou crownest the year with thy goodness and thy paths drop fatness. **Psalm 65:11**

There shall be a handful of corn in the earth upon the top of the mountains; the fruit thereof shall shake like Lebanon: and they of the city shall flourish like grass of the earth. **Psalm 72:16**

Thou hast caused men to ride over our heads; we went through fire and through water: but thou broughtest us out into a wealthy place. **Psalm 66:12**

And he said unto them, take heed, and beware of covetousness: for a man's life consisteth not in the abundance of the things which he possesseth. **Luke 12:15**

He that loveth silver shall not be satisfied with silver; nor he that loveth abundance with increase: this is also vanity. **Ecclesiastes 5:10**

28

INTRODUCTION ARMOR OF GOD/SPIRITUAL WARFARE

There are many attacks Satan and his legion of demons try to prevail against us, they have no power. We are truly in God's word and we are born-again. How can we resist the schemes of Satan, we have to pray and always be on our guard. There is spiritual warfare all around us, we have to be able to discern and detect when a battle could arise. This is why we need to put the full armor of God on daily, which is the breastplate of righteousness, the belt of truth, of the gospel of peace, the shield of faith, the helmet of salvation, and the sword of the spirit. We can't just put on the Armor of God when we think everything is okay that is when Satan and his demons come in and raise a battle against us.

When your guard is down then that is when the enemy comes in because we are vulnerable and are wide open to his attacks. The Armor of God must be put on daily. I put on God's armor every morning and pray to God that the schemes of the devil will not prevail in the mighty name of Jesus. If we are missing one piece of the Armor of God we are missing all of it. I encourage you when you wake up to pray in the spirit and put on the Full Armor of God to resist. The schemes of Satan and his demons' Spiritual warfare are very much real, some churches do not preach about it.

I am here to share with the nations and the churches that we should be preaching on it, teaching our people all about it, and preparing our people for battle and the spiritual forces of evil. That is in our world and all around us, to be alert and sober and always keep praying for God's people. The battles that will we soon be enduring here in America will get real. It's like a pimple that has been festering for a long time and it's about to pop. We used to be a Godly nation, now we are far off from God's word.

Do you have your armor on getting ready for battle on May 6th, 2024? I went through a battle that I knew Satan was not going to win. I am a part of the newspaper articles for the church section in my community. I wrote an article about hearing God's voice. I submitted the article on Sunday with a deadline of Tuesday. I got an email from the editor on Monday at 5:30 AM, saying, I couldn't open the file you sent me on my computer.

I was like, oh boy, here we go again, every time I get ready to send my article in for publishing, I endure a battle that Satan does not win. When I received the email I got up and turned on my Laptop. I was just going to print it off my email and take it to the newspaper business, when I printed it the paper got jammed. I took the paper out and guess what, it jammed again, it jammed three different times. I had to go to work soon, so I decided to go to the library during my lunchbreak to use their computer and printer. I got my email pulled up on their computer and I tried printing it, but I could not print it. I asked the librarian if they could help me.

He tried everything he could do to print it and he is brilliant with technology and he could not print it. I knew Satan was behind this, because he did not want this article to be published. Not to hear God's voice he will try everything he can to stop God's work. He has no power over God's people. On my way back to work, I prayed to God, 'Please, Father, let this article be published. I rebuke the schemes of the enemy please allow this to go through. Your work through me is very important to my community.' I take no credit for what God is doing through me it is all him doing the work, the battle I endured. With this article, spiritual warfare is at its finest but God's bigger than Satan's schemes.

The day then progressed still praying in the spirit against the schemes and attacks of Satan. I received an email from the editor at 10 PM, I was able to open your file, and it will be published. I shouted 'Hallelujah! Praise be to God, the one who fights our battles for us and gives us victory.' This is what happens when we put the full armor of God on, in the end, God wins. I was on cloud-nine because God came through and gave me victory over Satan's schemes.

A short while later, I went to sleep, I had a very interesting dream, in which I was prepping to become a martial arts point fighter. I used to be in taekwondo when I was younger, I hold a 2nd degree black belt, so, I know the bow ropes and have had a lot of training in my dream. I had a sparring helmet on, hand pads, footpads, and a chest plate protecting my chest, and I was wearing my black belt.

I don't remember much of this dream only that I was prepping for some kind of battle or training to spar or get ready to fight an opponent. The following day, while I was at work, I was really pondering and meditating on this dream. I have been out of taekwondo for about 25 years, so, I knew I was not going to get back into it or become a point fighter again. The Holy Spirit then spoke to me and gave me the interpretation of my dream. I am not prepping you to become a point fighter, I am prepping you for battle and spiritual warfare that we will soon endure here in America and God told me the martial arts gear I had on was the full Armor of God.

The Lord told me to add this topic and introduction to my book to share about putting the Full Armor of God on and Spiritual warfare. My book was nearly published, so, I reached out to my editor on May 7th, 2024. I have heard the Lord's voice and he wants me to add this topic to my book. If I had not gone through the battle that I went through over my newspaper article to get it published or had the dream about having the Full Armor of God on and prepping for battle and spiritual warfare, I would have not added this topic to my book.

God works in mysterious ways, you may have had God work in ways that you would have not ever thought he would work, but that is how our God works. I pray for the body of Christ to wake up and hold onto the hope God gives us through his son, Jesus Christ.

Half of the churches are sleeping right now, it's time to wake up and do what God has called us to and stop watering the word down as it has been for a long time. Is your armor on and all of it I would recommend putting it all on because the battles that we will go through here in America will soon get real.

God has been telling me to start prepping to be prepared for anything to come. Do churches even believe what the word says anymore? We have the power to cast out demons, it's not a gift it is a command. We have to fast and pray over casting demons out, after we cast out the demon we have to put something in its place or seven demons will come back even stronger. This is no joke, you have to know what you are doing because remember even the apostles had trouble casting demons out.

We have the power to raise the dead, we have the power to do anything the gifts of the Holy Spirit are in (1 Corinthians 12-14).

We can heal, pray in tongues, have the power to make the blind see, and the deaf hear, but remember this is God's power working through us, we are just his vessels, and we cannot do anything in our own strength or without Jesus (John 15:5).

Spiritual warfare is all around us and its real the lukewarm Christians may get swept away during the attacks that America will endure. I encourage you to get on fire for the lord and go out and proclaim his wonders and what he has done for you, share your testimony and lead people to the lord. Start a move of God before it's too late, and work out your salvation with fear and trembling (Philippians 2:12 KJV).

The day and hour are close to the Lord's return, wail for the day of the Lord is near, it will come like destruction from the almighty (Isaiah 13:6 KJV).

Make sure you're saved, because if you're not saved, it will be destruction upon you. Let's prep the body of Christ for battle and war. What does the world war mean? We are righteous to stand firm on the Word of God, his word endures forever (Isaiah 40:8 KJV).

It will withstand to the end of time, we as Christians are built on a solid foundation and his name is Jesus Christ, our Lord and Savior, we will not be shaken. However, the lukewarm Christian will be (Revelation 3:15-16 KJV).

34

Let's all join in unity and pray for nations to repent and put on the Full Armor of God to resist Satan and his demons (James 4:7).

SPIRITUAL WARFARE

What is spiritual warfare? It is the concept that refers to a battle between God's kingdom and Satan's kingdom. It is a conflict between light and darkness, in other words, a battle of good vs evil. For the Christian, it is the fight against the evil forces of rulers of darkness, powers, and spiritual wickedness. How do we fight and be victorious and win the battle against spiritual warfare? We have to rise up and stand up against the enemy, we have to be in constant prayer and worship, and remember the battle has already been won. When Jesus died on the cross, we had to be in fellowship with our brothers and sisters and go to church. We have to rebuke the schemes of the enemy; they have no power over us, but sometimes we give them power when our guard is down keep your eyes fixed on Jesus (Hebrews 12:2 KJV).

We have to conquer our fears, whatever that may be the Holy Spirit will enable us to conquer. Your battle, we all go through them, and some go through many it's how we react. Do not let the enemy gloat over you, do not give him any grounds to come in, and do not let him get his foot in when we sin and we continue to commit the same sin whatever it is, we give him a stronghold in our life. Be victorious, claim your victory, live in the moment you will conquer your spiritual battle. Keep your armor on to be victorious; we have to be in fellowship with one another. We cannot do this alone; we need

God's help and guidance from the Holy Spirit.

Spiritual warfare is all around us, and it's real. I often wonder how many churches actually preach on it or even know what it is. It's very important to know what it is and how to avoid it, and how to claim your victory. The United States is very much in spiritual warfare against the enemy. Satan is not hiding anymore. Some churches say it's ok to marry homosexuals in the church. No, it's not ok, it is an abomination against God's word, some churches are not even preaching sound doctrine, only giving itching ears (2 Timothy 4:3-4 KJV).

Oh, it's ok, I will condone your sin, we need to go back to our first love, that is Jesus Christ. The United States is on the edge of judgment. There are missionaries coming here now from overseas to preach to America that is unreal, we have become a mission field here in America. Some churches need to go back to their first love of preaching, sound doctrine, and the battles for the church will get real, but if a church is not in the Word, the spiritual warfare will get real. God is not happy with the way America has gone. We used to be a Godly nation, but this nation is far away from the gospel and sound teachings of the Word.

We need to go back to basic bible teachings. If a church marries homosexuals, they will be judged. If people are in a church, that sides with it I would strongly recommend getting out and finding a Bible. Teaching a church that will not water down the Word of God does not condone sin in a church. I used to go to a church that supported the agenda of marrying homosexuals, and I got out of that church. We need to pray for the churches, pray for the pastors to wake up, and repent for the ones who condone sin in the church. We need to pray for America and the nations; we need a touch from God here. In America, our nation is wicked and perverse, killing babies using drugs, the drinking that is going on, the human trafficking and sex trafficking that is happening in America, it is absolutely disgusting. God is crying for our nation here. Let's pray for this to stop, our youth are being targeted by the enemy, this is all spiritual warfare. Good vs Evil, God will not be mocked, His word will not return void (Isaiah 55:11 KJV).

I will be the first to go to my knees and repent of my sins. Remember, revival starts with us first and then goes elsewhere. The house of God is judged first, yes, that is us, Christians, the judgment starts with us. First, we need to clean our acts up and repent (Psalm 51:10 KJV). Let's keep focused on the word of God; there is nothing to worry about. God always wins, if our nation does not repent, we are in trouble. God may destroy America. We are becoming the modern-day Sodom and Gomorrah.

I am here to remind the body to pray and be focused on revival. If it happens, not prayer can change everything. I can see war and famine coming to America. Let's get prepared for battle, some of God's people, I am connected with, are telling people to stock up on food and water; it is not a bad idea. Look what is written in the book of Ezekiel 4:16-17, God told Ezekiel he was about to cut off the food supply in Jerusalem. The people will eat rationed food in anxiety and drink rationed water in despair, for food and water will be scarce; they will be appalled at the sight of each other and will waste away because of their sin. I know this is from the Old Testament days, but history may repeat itself. After reading this, look at our nation here in America, could that happen, food and water be scarce? I can see this happening.

Look what happened in March of 2020, we had a food shortage on the shelves. During that time, I was sick, I saw on social media about the toilet paper memes, and I was like, what was going on? I went to the store a week later, and everything was almost gone: no bread, no eggs, no toilet paper, and no hand sanitizer. This was all from the pandemic of COVID-19. I could not believe what I was seeing. Could this happen again? Absolutely, it can, I can see America going through another pandemic either before or after the election, only this time it will be worse.

Pray for America to repent and turn away from wickedness, or we will face judgment and destruction. We once were a Godly nation, but if we don't repent, we will be a heap of ruins. In the only testament, nations that turned away from God were destroyed; we are not far from that. Let's put on the Full Armor of God and battle the evil forces of darkness and prepare for spiritual warfare and battle. Keep the faith that was given to you by Jesus Christ, we will go through a battle here in America, nothing to worry about, God wins, keep your armor on. I have been battling a cold and a sore throat for about a week now.

Today is Sunday, May 12th, 2024. I was not planning to go to church because I didn't feel well. I woke up at 7 AM, and God told me to go to church. I'm surely glad I went because I had a powerful vision during the closing worship song.

In my vision, I was fully equipped with the armor of God. I was walking through the United States, and then I drove my sword into the ground. I went down on one knee and bowed down to our God. I looked up to the sky, then stood up, and the Lord lifted me into the air. I was above the United States, looking down on the land, and I saw dark clouds forming all over the borders of America—the East Coast, the West Coast, the Canadian border, and the southern border. The clouds then darkened even more, spreading across our nation, and covering all the states until they formed one big cloud over America.

Then the Lord spoke to me, saying, "Look up Amos 3:7: 'Surely the Lord God will do nothing, but He revealeth His secret to His servants the prophets.'" With this vision, the Lord revealed to me that America will darken even more. As the dark clouds continue to form, more darkness is to come upon our nation. We need to pray for America. Only a remnant will be left. This is a Word from the Lord to His servant, Joshua, as we endure more spiritual warfare.

I encourage you to keep your armor on. Resist the devil and his schemes. To keep it on, we have to do our part—only you can do this; no one can do it for you except God. This is between God and you. Keep your armor on, and remain steadfast in God's Word. We will go through a battle zone here in America. Will we rise up and stand against this darkness to come, or will the church be lukewarm and do nothing? I will rise up, whether this takes my life or not. God will not be mocked. God's Word endures forever (Isaiah 40:8 KJV).

Will we fight against our enemy and prevail? Do not let the enemy have a foothold in your life. Rebuke the schemes of Satan. Do not let your foundation have a crack in it. The sin that we commit repeatedly, that we do nothing about, opens the crack even more. You're probably wondering what the picture of the fire is all about. If you look closely, you can see a dragon protruding out. You can see the eyes, the head, the fins on the neck, and the tail. It resembles Satan. He is not hiding in America or the nation.

41

I took this picture of the fire in June of 2021 while I was camping here in Iowa, three years ago. This is how real the situation in America has become, and it will get worse. The Bible says it will get darker and darker. Keep your armor on and fight your battles with authority in the mighty, everlasting name of Jesus. The gates of hell will not prevail. What are the odds of capturing a dragon that resembles Satan on camera? There are no odds—look at how real the situation in America has become and how evil our nation is.

Let's stand up to the enemy and fight our battles. The battle has already been won. God wins all the time. Spiritual warfare is real, and we can win the battle only through Jesus Christ. We have victory. I have learned a lot in five short years. I pray that I can continue to keep the faith and win the battles. I also pray for others to keep their faith. I have learned to just let things go and let God do the work. Do not take matters into your own hands; let God fight the battle for you. I have done that, and all it does is create enemies. When we let God do the work and fight our battles for us, then we get victory.

How have you gone through a spiritual battle? Was your armor on?

Prayer

'Dear heavenly Father, I come boldly to Your throne of grace. I pray, Father, that people can keep the faith even as this world grows darker and more evil comes. I pray, Father, that the body of Christ will remain steadfast in Your Word, I pray Father for the people here in the nations, for the battles we will endure, and that we will always look to You and keep You number one in our lives. Father, please be with us as we prepare for battle and war against the enemy. Father, give us mercy and grace as we prepare for spiritual warfare. Here in the nations, we will not fade or crumble. I cry out for the people to repent and turn to You. I cry out to You, Father, for the nations to repent. My heart pours out for my country and nation of the United States and all the rest of the nations in Jesus Christ's name. I pray. Amen.'

ARMOR OF GOD/SPIRITUAL WARFARE

Finally, my brethren, be strong in the Lord, and in the power of His might.

Put on the whole armor of God, that ye may be able to stand against the wiles of the devil.

For we wrestle not against flesh and blood, but against principalities, against powers, against the rulers of the darkness of this world, against spiritual wickedness in high places.

Wherefore take unto you the whole armor of God, that ye may be able to withstand in the evil day, and having done all, to stand.

Stand, therefore, having your loins girt about with truth, and having on the breastplate of righteousness;

And your feet shod with the preparation of the gospel of peace;

Above all, taking the shield of faith, wherewith ye shall be able to quench all the fiery darts of the wicked.

And take the helmet of salvation, and the sword of the Spirit, which is the word of God:

Praying always with all prayer and supplication in the Spirit, and watching thereunto with all perseverance and supplication for all saints;

And for me, that utterance may be given unto me, that I may open my mouth boldly, to make known the mystery of the gospel,

For which I am an ambassador in bonds: that therein I may speak boldly, as I ought to speak. **Ephesians 6:10-20**

For he put on righteousness as a breastplate, and a helmet of salvation upon his head; and he put on the garments of vengeance for clothing and was clad with zeal as a cloak. **Isaiah 59:17**

By the word of truth, by the power of God, by the armor of righteousness on the right hand and on the left. **2 Corinthians 6:7**

(For the weapons of our warfare are not carnal, but mighty through God to the pulling down of strongholds ;)

Casting down imaginations, and every high thing that exalteth itself against the knowledge of God, and bringing into captivity every thought to the obedience of Christ. **2 Corinthians 10:4-5**

Therefore, let us not sleep, as do others; but let us watch and be sober.

For they that sleep in the night; and they that be drunken are drunken in the night.

But let us, who are of the day, be sober, putting on the breastplate of faith and love; and for a helmet, the hope of salvation. **1 Thessalonians 5:6-8**

And the God of peace shall bruise Satan under your feet shortly. The grace of our Lord Jesus Christ is with you. Amen. **Romans 16:20**

For the eyes of the Lord are over the righteous, and his ears are open unto their prayers: but the face of the Lord is against them that do evil.

And who is he that will harm you, if ye be followers of that which is good?

But and if ye suffer for righteousness sake, happy are ye: and be not afraid of their terror, neither be troubled. **1 Peter 3:12-14**

For whatsoever is born of God overcometh the world: and this is the victory that overcometh the world, even our faith.

Who is he that overcometh the world, but he that believeth that Jesus is the Son of God? **1 John 5:4-5**

Blessed are they that keep judgment, and he that doeth righteousness at all times. **Psalm 106:3**

The night is far spent, the day is at hand: let us therefore cast off the works of darkness and let us put on the armor of light.

Let us walk honestly, as in the day; not in rioting and drunkenness, not in chambering and wantonness, not in strife and envying.

But put ye on the Lord Jesus Christ, and make not provision for the flesh, to fulfill the lusts thereof. **Romans 13:12-14**

But and if ye suffer for righteousness sake, happy are ye: and be not afraid of their terror, neither be troubled. **1 Peter 3:14**

And righteousness shall be the girdle of his loins, and faithfulness the girdle of his reins. **Isaiah 11:5**

Lest Satan should get an advantage of us: for we are not ignorant of his devices. **2 Corinthians 2:11**

Then saith Jesus unto him, get thee hence, Satan: for it is written, Thou, shalt worship the Lord thy God, and him only shalt thou serve. **Matthews 4:10**

Be sober, be vigilant; because your adversary the devil, as a roaring lion, walketh about, seeking whom he may devour: Whom resist steadfast in the faith, knowing that the same afflictions are accomplished in your brethren that are in the world. **1 Peter 5:8-9**

Now we command you, brethren, in the name of our Lord Jesus Christ, that ye withdraw yourselves from every brother that walketh disorderly, and not after the tradition which he received of us. **2 Thessalonians 3:6**

Whereunto he called you by our gospel, to the obtaining of the glory of our Lord Jesus Christ.

Therefore, brethren, stand fast and hold the traditions which ye have been taught, whether by word, or our epistle. **2 Thessalonians 2:14-15**

Because the carnal mind is enmity against God: for it is not subject to the law of God, neither indeed can be. **Romans 8:7**

Therefore, let us not sleep, as do others; but let us watch and be sober. **1 Thessalonians 5:6**

And God saw that the wickedness of man was great in the earth and that every imagination of the thoughts of his heart was only evil continually. **Genesis 6:5**

Knowing this first, that there shall come in the last days scoffers, walking after their own lusts,

And saying, Where is the promise of his coming? for since the fathers fell asleep, all things continue as they were from the beginning of the creation. **2 Peter 3:3-4**

Who hath delivered us from the power of darkness, and hath

translated us into the kingdom of his dear Son. **Colossians 1:13**

And he said unto them, I beheld Satan as lightning fall from heaven.

Behold, I give unto you the power to tread on serpents and scorpions, and over all the power of the enemy: and nothing shall by any means hurt you.

Notwithstanding in this rejoice not, that the spirits are subject unto you; but rather rejoice, because your names are written in heaven. **Luke 10:18-20**

The LORD shall cause thine enemies that rise up against thee to be smitten before thy face: they shall come out against thee one way, and flee before thee seven ways. **Deuteronomy 28:7**

And no marvel; for Satan himself is transformed into an angel of light. **2 Corinthians 11:14**

No weapon that is formed against thee shall prosper; and every tongue that shall rise against thee in judgment thou shalt condemn. This is the heritage of the servants of the LORD, and their righteousness is of me, saith the LORD. **Isaiah 54:17**

Verily I say unto you, Whatsoever ye shall bind on earth shall be bound in heaven: and whatsoever ye shall loose on earth shall be loosed in heaven.

Again I say unto you, That if two of you shall agree on earth as touching anything that they shall ask, it shall be done for them of my Father which is in heaven.

For where two or three are gathered together in my name, there am I in the midst of them. **Matthew 18:18-20**

And there was war in heaven: Michael and his angels fought against the dragon, and the dragon fought and his angels,

And prevailed not; neither was their place found any more in heaven.

And the great dragon was cast out, that old serpent, called the Devil, and Satan, which deceiveth the whole world: he was cast out into the earth, and his angels were cast out with him. **Revelation 12:7-9**

Nay, in all these things we are more than conquerors through him who loved us. **Romans 8:37**

Forasmuch then as the children are partakers of flesh and blood, he also himself likewise took part of the same; that through death he might

destroy him that had the power of death, that is, the devil. **Hebrews 2:14**

Thou believest that there is one God; thou doest well: the devils also believe, and tremble. **James 2:19**

For with God, nothing shall be impossible. **Luke 1:37**

The wicked plotteth against the just, and gnasheth upon him with his teeth.

The LORD shall laugh at him: for he seeth that his day is coming.

The wicked have drawn out the sword, and have bent their bow, to cast down the poor and needy, and to slay such as be of upright conversation.

Their sword shall enter into their own heart, and their bows shall be broken.

A little that a righteous man hath is better than the riches of many wicked. **Psalm 37:12-16**

And I say also unto thee, That thou art Peter, and upon this rock I will build my church; and the gates of hell shall not prevail against it. **Matthew 16:18**

They compassed me about like bees: they are quenched as the fire of thorns: for in the name of the LORD, I will destroy them.

Thou hast thrust sore at me that I might fall: but the LORD helped me. **Psalm 118:12-13**

Even him, whose coming is after the working of Satan with all power and signs and lying wonders,

And with all deceivableness of unrighteousness in them that perish; because they received not the love of the truth, that they might be saved. **2 Thessalonians 2:9-10**

Therefore rejoice, ye heavens, and ye that dwell in them. Woe to the inhabitors of the earth and of the sea! For the devil is come down unto you, having great wrath, because he knoweth that he hath but a short time. **Revelation 12:12**

Ye are of your father the devil, and the lusts of your father ye will do. He was a murderer from the beginning, and abode not in the truth because there is no truth in him. When he speaketh a lie, he speaketh of his own: for he is a liar and the father of it. **John 8:44**

These shall make war with the Lamb, and the Lamb shall overcome them: for he is Lord of lords and King of kings: and they that are with him are called, and chosen, and faithful. **Revelation 17:14**

When thou passest through the waters, I will be with thee; and through the rivers, they shall not overflow thee: when thou walkest through the fire, thou shalt not be burned; neither shall the flame kindle upon thee. **Isaiah 43:2**

And having spoiled principalities and powers, he made a shew of them openly, triumphing over them in it. **Colossians 2:15**

And lead us not into temptation, but deliver us from evil: For thine is the kingdom, and the power, and the glory, forever. Amen. **Matthew 6:13**

Ye shall not fear them: for the LORD your God, he shall fight for you. **Deuteronomy 3:22**

But thanks be to God, which giveth us the victory through our Lord Jesus Christ. **1 Corinthians 15:57**

I know thy works, and tribulation, and poverty, (but thou art rich) and I know the blasphemy of them which say they are Jews and are not, but are the synagogue of Satan. **Revelation 2:9**

But the Lord is faithful, who shall establish you, and keep you from evil. **2 Thessalonians 3:3**

Let us draw near with a true heart in full assurance of faith, having our hearts sprinkled from an evil conscience, and our bodies washed with pure water. **Hebrews 10:22**

He disappointeth the devices of the crafty so that their hands cannot perform their enterprise. **Job 5:12**

He that committeth sin is of the devil; for the devil sinneth from the beginning. For this purpose, the Son of God was manifested, that he might destroy the works of the devil. **1 John 3:8**

Watch ye, stand fast in the faith, quit you like men, be strong. 1 Corinthians 16:13

Hast thou not known? hast thou not heard, that the everlasting God, the LORD, the Creator of the ends of the earth, fainteth not, neither is weary? there is no searching of his understanding.

He giveth power to the faint; and to them that have no might he increaseth strength.

Even the youths shall faint and be weary, and the young men shall utterly fall:

But they that wait upon the LORD shall renew their strength; they shall mount up with wings as eagles; they shall run, and not be weary; and they shall walk, and not faint. **Isaiah 40:28-31**

This I say then, Walk in the Spirit, and ye shall not fulfill the lust of the flesh.

For the flesh lusteth against the Spirit, and the Spirit against the flesh: and these are contrary the one to the other: so that ye cannot do the things that ye would. **Galatians 5:16-17**

And I heard a loud voice saying in heaven, Now is come salvation and strength, and the kingdom of our God, and the power of his

Christ: for the accuser of our brethren is cast down, which accused them before our God day and night. **Revelation 12:10**

Behold, I will make them of the synagogue of Satan, which say they are Jews and are not, but do lie; behold, I will make them to come and worship before thy feet, and to know that I have loved thee. **Revelation 3:9**

Now is the judgment of this world: now shall the prince of this world be cast out. **John 12:31**

And the Lord shall deliver me from every evil work and will preserve me unto his heavenly kingdom: to whom be glory forever and ever. Amen. **2 Timothy 4:18**

Through thee will we push down our enemies: through thy name will we tread them under that rise up against us. **Psalm 44:5**

And it came to pass, when the ark set forward, that Moses said, Rise up, LORD, and let thine enemies be scattered; and let them that hate thee flee before thee. **Numbers 10:35**

For thou hast been a strength to the poor, a strength to the needy in his distress, a refuge from the storm, a shadow from the heat when the blast of the terrible ones is as a storm against the wall.

Thou shalt bring down the noise of strangers, as the heat in a dry place; even the heat with the shadow of a cloud: the branch of the terrible ones shall be brought low. **Isaiah 25:4-5**

It is better to trust in the LORD than to put confidence in princes.

All nations compassed me about: but in the name of the LORD will I destroy them.

They compassed me about; yea, they compassed me about: but in the name of the LORD I will destroy them. **Psalm 118:9-11**

I know thy works, that thou art neither cold nor hot: I would thou wert cold or hot.

So then because thou art lukewarm, and neither cold nor hot, I will spue thee out of my mouth. **Revelation 3:15-16**

And if a house be divided against itself, that house cannot stand.

And if Satan rises up against himself, and be divided, he cannot stand but hath an end.

No man can enter into a strong man's house, and spoil his goods, except he will first bind the strong man; and then he will spoil his house.

Verily I say unto you, All sins shall be forgiven unto the sons of men, and blasphemies wherewith soever they shall blaspheme:

But he that shall blaspheme against the Holy Ghost hath never forgiveness but is in danger of eternal damnation.

Because they said, He hath an unclean spirit.

There came then his brethren and his mother, and, standing without, sent unto him, calling him. **Mark 3:25-30**

INTRODUCTION BLESSINGS

The blessings God gives us are so great, He blesses us beyond measure. We have to put God first and live a Godly life; if we don't live a life pleasing to God, he will not bless us. The blessings He has given me are amazing. God wants us to walk in obedience with Him, and the blessings that follow are plentiful. How has the Lord blessed you? I'm sure it brings you to tears, how the lord has blessed you. The tears of joy that run down my face when blessings arise give me assurance. God is with me when you get blessings, take time to give thanks to Jesus, thanks and praise for what He has done for us.

How has the Lord given you blessings when we put him first?

Prayer

'Loving Father, we strive to be obedient to Your Word. Please bless us, when we put You first and obey Your commands, help us to always remain in You as the blessings flow.'

BLESSINGS

Blessed be the God and Father of our Lord Jesus Christ, who hath blessed us with all spiritual blessings in heavenly places in Christ. **Ephesians 1:3**

Blessed is every one that feareth the LORD; that walketh in his ways. **Psalms 128:1**

The LORD bless thee, and keep thee:

The LORD make his face shine upon thee, and be gracious unto thee:

The LORD lift up his countenance upon thee and give thee peace. **Numbers 6:24-26**

Give, and it shall be given unto you; good measure, pressed down, and shaken together, and running over, shall men give into your bosom. For with the same measure that ye mete withal it shall be measured to you again. **Luke 6:38**

Bring ye all the tithes into the storehouse, that there may be meat in mine house, and prove me now herewith, saith the LORD of hosts, if I will not open you the windows of heaven, and pour you out a blessing, that there shall not be room enough to receive it. **Malachi 3:10**

Blessed are they that mourn: for they shall be comforted. **Matthew 5:4**

But my God shall supply all your needs according to his riches in glory by Christ Jesus. **Philippians 4:19**

God shall bless us, and all the ends of the earth shall fear him. **Psalms 67:7**

Every good gift and every perfect gift is from above, and cometh down from the Father of lights, with whom is no variableness, neither shadow of turning. **James 1:17**

And said, By myself have I sworn, saith the LORD, for because thou hast done this thing, and hast not withheld thy son, thine only son:

That in blessing I will bless thee, and in multiplying I will multiply thy seed as the stars of the heaven, and as the sand which is upon the sea shore; and thy seed shall possess the gate of his enemies. **Genesis 22:16-17**

Blessed is the man that walketh not in the counsel of the ungodly, nor standeth in the way of sinners, nor sitteth in the seat of the scornful.

But his delight is in the law of the LORD; and in his law doth he meditate day and night.

And he shall be like a tree planted by the rivers of water, that bringeth forth his fruit in his season; his leaf also shall not wither; and whatsoever he doeth shall prosper. **Psalms 1:1-3**

And God is able to make all grace abound toward you; that ye, always having all sufficiency in all things, may abound to every good work. **2nd Corinthians 9:8**

For I will pour water upon him that is thirsty, and floods upon the dry ground: I will pour my spirit upon thy seed, and my blessing upon thine offspring. **Isaiah 44:3**

BE STILL

For many believers, being still is hard. God wants us to rest in Him and to know how to trust Him. Trusting God's plan requires us to be still and know He is God (Psalm 46:10). Being calm and still requires a lot of patience, knowing God will help us to remain still in times of quietness.

God wants you to know that in times of stillness is when we hear His voice (Ezekiel 1:25). When we are in total stillness, God speaks to us directly, whether through His voice or through the Word. The Holy Spirit enables us to remain still. Allow yourself to reflect on the Scriptures to remain still and calm.

I can recall a time in my life when I was running around stir-crazy, and the Holy Spirit tugged on me, assuring me that everything would be okay. The busyness of the world distracts us from the quiet times God wants us to spend with Him. How much time do we really spend with God? I fail at this at times. God wants us to be in fellowship with Him. When we are still, God comes through and speaks to us directly (Psalm 68:33).

Allow the Holy Spirit to help you remain still, and God will hold you tight and love you. He wants your attention. During the quiet times, He speaks to us and shows us things we need to work on.

Allow the Holy Spirit to help you remain calm in busy times. God loves you, my friend, and the Holy Spirit will guide you in the still and quiet times during our journey with Jesus Christ—a road to victory. Remain still, and God will shine brightly in your walk with Jesus.

How can you remain still and calm during the busyness of a world that is noisy?

Prayer

'Heavenly Father, thank You for being with us during the still and quiet times of our lives. Please, Father, show me ways to remain still in a busy world. Please, Father, show us Your grace and mercy in a busy world that distracts us from the peace and stillness that You want us to have. We ask You, Father, to continue to show us how to remain still and remain in You in Jesus Christ's name. We pray. Amen.'

INTRODUCTION BAPTISM OF THE HOLY SPIRIT

How do we receive the Baptism of the Holy Spirit? One should seek it. God wants all believers to be baptized in the Holy Spirit. All we have to do to receive this is ask for it. You can receive it by the laying on of hands, having someone pray over you to receive it, or you can receive it by praying. All you have to do is ask for it, and the power of the Holy Spirit will come upon you.

This is different from water baptism, which is an inward change and an outward dedication to our faith—a public declaration of our faith in Christ. The initial evidence of the Baptism of the Holy Spirit is speaking in tongues.

How did I receive the Baptism of the Holy Spirit? I was watching a YouTube video about the Baptism of the Holy Spirit, and the preacher asked, "Are you ready to receive this?" I raised my hands in the air and declared, "Jesus Christ is Lord and Savior." I asked God for it because I wanted it. We have to want it—God won't give us something that we don't desire. If we do want the Baptism of the Holy Spirit, the Lord will give it to us.

The fire of God came upon me, and I started speaking in tongues. The gifts of the Holy Spirit soon began manifesting in my ministry.

Not long after I received the Baptism of the Holy Spirit, I started seeing signs and wonders. The power of the Holy Spirit and the fire of God manifested greatly in my life and ministry. There were many times God gave me a scripture that related either to what I was going through or to someone else.

My son has this gift too. He operates in signs and wonders, words of wisdom, revelation, and knowledge. God has used him to keep me on track, and I give God all the glory. We share the same gifts of the Holy Spirit, and He will use us mightily together—even though my son is only 16, the power of the Holy Spirit is upon him.

We have to seek and desire the Baptism of the Holy Spirit. God will give it to us—all we have to do is ask for it. He will baptize you with the Holy Spirit and with fire, a radiant fire that only comes from God. The Lord will give it to you if you ask.

The Baptism of the Holy Spirit is different from receiving the Holy Spirit. When we receive the Holy Spirit, that is Jesus coming into us as we repent and invite Him into our hearts (Acts 2:38 KJV). That is when the gift of the Holy Spirit comes into us—that is Jesus. The Baptism of the Holy Spirit is the infilling of the Holy Spirit. Do you want to operate more with the fire of God? All you have to do is pray and ask for it. I pray that you will desire this and receive it.

Have you received the Baptism of the Holy Spirit? Do you speak in tongues? Do you operate in signs and wonders? Has the Fire of God come upon you once you have received this? I pray for you that you will have this wonderful gift.

Prayer

'Dear heavenly Father, I pray for those who are reading this that they will receive the Baptism of the Holy Spirit. I pray, Father, that all believers will want this precious gift of Your fire and power to bring people to You in Jesus Christ's mighty name. I pray, amen, and amen, the Fire of God will be upon You once You want this and receive it. I declare in the everlasting mighty name of Jesus, Holy one of Israel, Your church is on fire to spread the gospel to the nations.'

BAPTISM OF THE HOLY SPIRIT

I indeed baptize you with water unto repentance. But he that cometh after me is mightier than I, whose shoes I am not worthy to bear: he shall baptize you with the Holy Ghost, and with fire. **Matthew 3:11**

And, being assembled together with them, commanded them that they should not depart from Jerusalem, but wait for the promise of the Father, which, saith he, ye have heard of me.

For John truly baptized with water, but ye shall be baptized with the Holy Ghost not many days hence. **Acts 1:4-5**

And when they had prayed, the place was shaken where they were assembled together; and they were all filled with the Holy Ghost, and they spake the word of God with boldness. **Acts 4:31**

But ye shall receive power, after that the Holy Ghost comes upon you: and ye shall be witnesses unto me both in Jerusalem, and in all Judaea, and in Samaria, and unto the uttermost part of the earth. **Acts 1:8**

John answered, saying unto them all, I indeed baptize you with water; but one mightier than I cometh, the latchet of whose shoes I am not worthy to unloose: he shall baptize you with the Holy Ghost and with fire. **Luke 3:16**

And they were all filled with the Holy Ghost and began to speak with other tongues, as the Spirit gave them utterance. **Acts 2:4**

And I knew him not: but he that sent me to baptize with water, the same said unto me, Upon, whom thou shalt see the Spirit descending, and remaining on him, the same is he which baptizeth with the Holy Ghost. **John 1:33**

I indeed have baptized you with water: but he shall baptize you with the Holy Ghost. **Mark 1:8**

And be not drunk with wine, wherein is excess; but be filled with the Spirit. **Ephesians 5:18**

And when Paul had laid his hands upon them, the Holy Ghost came on them; and they spake with tongues, and prophesied. **Acts 19:6**

But the Comforter, which is the Holy Ghost, whom the Father will send in my name, he shall teach you all things, and bring all things to your remembrance, whatsoever I have said unto you. **John 14:26**

Now, when the apostles which were at Jerusalem heard that Samaria had received the word of God, they sent unto them Peter and John:

Who, when they were come down, prayed for them, that they might receive the Holy Ghost:

(For as yet he was fallen upon none of them: only they were

baptized in the name of the Lord Jesus.)

Then laid they their hands on them, and they received the Holy Ghost. **Acts 8:14-17**

Then said Paul, John verily baptized with the baptism of repentance, saying unto the people, that they should believe on him which should come after him, that is, on Christ Jesus. **Acts 19:4**

But ye, beloved, building up yourselves on your most holy faith, praying in the Holy Ghost. **Jude 20**

While Peter yet spake these words, the Holy Ghost fell on all of them who heard the word.

And they of the circumcision which believed were astonished, as many as came with Peter, because that on the Gentiles also was poured out the gift of the Holy Ghost.

For they heard them speak with tongues, and magnify God. Then answered Peter. **Acts 10:44-46**

And Ananias went his way, and entered into the house; and putting his hands on him said, Brother Saul, the Lord, even Jesus, that appeared unto thee in the way as thou camest, hath sent me, that thou mightest receive thy sight, and be filled with the Holy Ghost. **Acts 9:17**

How God anointed Jesus of Nazareth with the Holy Ghost and with power: who went about doing good, and healing all that were oppressed of the devil; for God was with him. **Acts 10:38**

And as I began to speak, the Holy Ghost fell on them, as on us at the beginning.

Then remembered I the word of the Lord, how that he said, John indeed baptized with water; but ye shall be baptized with the Holy Ghost. **Acts 11:15-16**

And John bare record, saying, I saw the Spirit descending from heaven like a dove, and it abode upon him.

And I knew him not: but he that sent me to baptize with water, the same said unto me, Upon, whom thou shalt see the Spirit descending, and remaining on him, the same is he which baptizeth with the Holy Ghost.

And I saw, and bare record that this is the Son of God. **John 1:32-34**

And Jesus being full of the Holy Ghost returned from Jordan and was led by the Spirit into the wilderness. **Luke 4:1**

And suddenly there came a sound from heaven as of a rushing mighty wind, and it filled all the house where they were sitting.

And there appeared unto them cloven tongues like as of fire, and it sat upon each of them. **Acts 2:2-3**

For he that speaketh in an unknown tongue speaketh not unto men, but unto God: for no man understandeth him; howbeit in the spirit he speaketh mysteries. **1 Corinthians 14:2**

Then Saul, (who also is called Paul,) filled with the Holy Ghost, set his eyes on him. **Acts 13:9**

But he, being full of the Holy Ghost, looked up steadfastly into heaven, and saw the glory of God, and Jesus standing on the right hand of God. **Acts 7:55**

INTRODUCTION COURAGE

Courage is what we need in this dying world to step out of our comfort zone and share the gospel with the lost. It's not easy to have the courage to do this, but it's necessary. Gideon lacked the courage to move forward; he doubted his ability to do what God called him to do (Judges 6-8 KJV). An angel of the Lord appeared to him to save Israel from the hands of the Midianites. The Lord used Gideon to defeat them. Where is our courage to stand up for what is right? If God can use Gideon, even when he feels weak, God will use us for His glory. Take the courage to do what God has called us to do.

Was there a time in your life when you needed courage to do the will of the Father?

Prayer

'Heavenly Father, please give us the courage to stand up for what is right, when we feel weak, please give us the strength and the courage to move forward in our ministry.'

COURAGE

Be strong and of good courage, fear not, nor be afraid of them: for the LORD thy God, he it is that doth go with thee; he will not fail thee, nor forsake thee.

And Moses called unto Joshua, and said unto him in the sight of all Israel, Be strong and of good courage: for thou must go with this people unto the land which the LORD hath sworn unto their fathers to give them; and thou shalt cause them to inherit it.

And the LORD, he it is that doth go before thee; he will be with thee, he will not fail thee, neither forsake thee: fear not, neither be dismayed. **Deuteronomy 31:6-8**

Finally, my brethren, be strong in the Lord, and in the power of his might. **Ephesians 6:10**

Fear not; for thou shalt not be ashamed: neither be thou confounded; for thou shalt not be put to shame: for thou shalt forget the shame of thy youth, and shalt not remember the reproach of thy widowhood any more. **Isaiah 54:4**

The LORD is my light and my salvation; whom shall I fear? the LORD is the strength of my life; of whom shall I be afraid? **Psalm 27:1**

For God hath not given us the spirit of fear; but of power, and of love, and of a sound mind. **2 Timothy 1:7**

Have not I commanded thee? Be strong and of good courage; be not afraid, neither be thou dismayed: for the LORD thy God is with thee whithersoever thou goest. **Joshua 1:9**

Watch ye, stand fast in the faith, quit you like men, be strong. **1 Corinthians 16:13**

As soon as Jesus heard the word that was spoken, he saith unto the ruler of the synagogue, Be not afraid, only believe. Mark 5:36

And in nothing terrified by your adversaries: which is to them an evident token of perdition, but to you of salvation, and that of God. **Philippians 1:28**

He shall not be afraid of evil tidings: his heart is fixed, trusting in the LORD. **Psalm 112:7**

Be of good courage, and he shall strengthen your heart, all ye that hope in the LORD. **Psalm 31:24**

Fear thou not; for I am with thee: be not dismayed; for I am thy God: I will strengthen thee; yea, I will help thee; yea, I will uphold thee with the right hand of my righteousness. **Isaiah 41:10**

But when they saw him walking upon the sea, they supposed it had been a spirit, and cried out:

For they all saw him and were troubled. And immediately he talked with them, and saith unto them, Be of good cheer: it is I; be not afraid. **Mark 6:49-50**

INTRODUCTION CHRISTS COMING

Jesus will indeed return to earth. He will come down, not on a donkey, but from heaven on a white horse, with His mighty angels surrounding Him. I believe the rapture will happen first, then the tribulation, during which the Holy Spirit will be taken away from this earth. I believe the tribulation will last seven years, and during this time, people will still have a choice to receive Jesus. This is why I mentioned in the Eternal Life topic the importance of leaving letters behind for the survivors of the rapture, to teach them how to receive Jesus and how to lead others to the Lord.

After the tribulation will be the millennium when Christ establishes His kingdom on earth for 1,000 years. Those who are in Christ will come down from heaven with Jesus. I strongly believe this will happen, though we could be wrong, as there are many beliefs about how the Book of Revelation will play out. I preach to be prepared at all times, as it will come like a thief in the night.

I believe Revelation 1-4 is about the church, Revelation 5-19 is about the tribulation, and Revelation 20 is about the millennium, which will last 1,000 years. Satan will be bound for those 1,000 years, and when the period is over, he will be released from his prison for a short while to deceive the nations in the four corners of the earth—Gog and Magog—to gather them for battle. Fire will then devour them. This is the final battle against God's people. The devil will then be cast into the lake of fire, where the beast and the false prophet have been thrown (Revelation 20:7-10 KJV). They will be tormented day and night forever.

The Book of Life will be opened, and the names that are not found in it will go to hell (Revelation 20:11-15 KJV). Make absolutely sure that your name is on it. Ensure your salvation is secure by repenting, asking for forgiveness of your sins, and inviting Jesus to come into your heart. If you have not done this, you will go to hell. I write to you in love to receive Jesus to escape the depths of hell.

Revelation 21 speaks of the new heaven, the new earth, and the new Jerusalem. This is what I believe in a nutshell: Rapture first, with the Battle of Armageddon (Revelation 16:16 KJV) occurring during the tribulation period. After that is over, the millennium takes place, then the War of Gog and Magog, which is Satan's final battle against God's people. After the war, the Book of Life is sealed and closed. Anyone whose name is not in it is cast into the lake of fire. Then comes the new heaven, the new earth, and the new Jerusalem. God wins, and He always will win. The battle has already been won.

Where will you be when Christ returns? With Him or without Him? Choose this day whom you will serve (Joshua 24:15 KJV). We can't serve two masters; it's either Jesus or Satan. We can't serve both. I hope you are with Jesus.

Where will America be in all of this? I really don't know. Will our nation be destroyed? Will we join forces with other nations before the rapture? I don't know; I don't have an answer for that. I believe our nation will be judged by God soon. We are a modern-day Babylon. I have had many dreams about this nation that will be written about in another topic. I do believe judgment is coming. Could we go through another pandemic worse than COVID-19? I believe so. I believe persecution is coming to America like we have never seen. Some will be killed for their faith in Jesus. Will we die for Jesus, or will we deny Him? Or will we endure until the end? (Revelation 2:26 KJV; Matthew 24:13 KJV).

Those who are saved will be raptured, and we will be in heaven with Jesus during the tribulation. So, who knows what will happen to America? I don't know. I can see some revival coming here before we depart. I believe there will be lots of revival during the tribulation and that the 1,000 years when Jesus establishes His kingdom on earth will be glorious. It will be peace on earth. I am here to share my love for Jesus with the nations. Be secure in your faith.

Where will you be when Christ returns to earth with or without him?

Prayer

'Dear heavenly Father, we thank You for Your Word, Your Word endures forever. We ask You, Father, to give us peace while we eagerly await your return.'

CHRIST'S COMING

But of that day and hour knoweth no man, no, not the angels of heaven, but my Father only. **Matthew 24:36**

Therefore, be ye also ready: for in such an hour as ye think not the Son of man cometh. **Matthew 24:44**

Watch, therefore, for ye know neither the day nor the hour wherein the Son of man cometh. **Matthew 25:13**

So, Christ was once offered to bear the sins of many; and unto them that look for him shall he appear the second time without sin unto salvation. **Hebrews 9:28**

And I saw thrones, and they sat upon them, and judgment was given unto them: and I saw the souls of them that were beheaded for the witness of Jesus, and for the word of God, and which had not worshipped the beast, neither his image, neither had received his mark upon their foreheads, nor in their hands; and they lived and reigned with Christ a thousand years. **Revelation 20:4**

For yourselves know perfectly that the day of the Lord so cometh as a thief in the night. **1 Thessalonians 5:2**

Behold, he cometh with clouds; and every eye shall see him, and they also which pierced him: and all kindreds of the earth shall wail because of him. Even so, Amen. **Revelation 1:7**

And now, little children, abide in him; that, when he shall appear, we may have confidence, and not be ashamed before him at his coming. **1 John 2:28**

And, behold, I come quickly; and my reward is with me, to give every man according as his work shall be. **Revelation 22:12**

In a moment, in the twinkling of an eye, at the last trump: for the trumpet shall sound, and the dead shall be raised incorruptible, and we shall be changed. **1 Corinthians 15:52**

Be ye therefore ready also: for the Son of man cometh at an hour when ye think not. **Luke 12:40**

For the Lord himself shall descend from heaven with a shout, with the voice of the archangel, and with the trump of God: and the dead in Christ shall rise first:

Then we which are alive and remain shall be caught up together with them in the clouds, to meet the Lord in the air: and so, shall we ever be with the Lord. **1 Thessalonians 4:16-17**

Looking for that blessed hope, and the glorious appearance of the great God and our Saviour Jesus Christ. **Titus 2:13**

For the Son of man shall come in the glory of his Father with his angels and then he shall reward every man according to his works. **Matthew 16:27**

Behold, I come quickly: hold that fast which thou hast, that no man take thy crown. **Revelation 3:11**

Henceforth there is laid up for me a crown of righteousness, which the Lord, the righteous judge, shall give me at that day: and not to me only, but unto all them also that love his appearing**. 2 Timothy 4:8**

Which also said, Ye men of Galilee, why stand ye gazing up into heaven? this same Jesus, which is taken up from you into heaven, shall so come in like manner as ye have seen him go into heaven. **Acts 1:11**

And as he sat upon the mount of Olives, the disciples came unto him privately, saying, Tell us, when shall these things be? and what shall be the sign of thy coming, and of the end of the world? **Matthew 24:3**

When Christ, who is our life, shall appear, then shall ye also appear with him in glory. **Colossians 3:4**

And then shall that Wicked be revealed, whom the Lord shall consume with the spirit of his mouth, and shall destroy with the brightness of his coming. **2 Thessalonians 2:8**

CHARACTER

DAILY READING ROMANS 8:1-14

Character is an important aspect of who we are in Christ. Our actions can harm our witness, especially when we claim to be Christians but behave no differently than the world around us. Such inconsistency damages our character and sends a confusing message. How can we expect others to believe in the power of Christ if our lives don't reflect His teachings? When the world looks at us and sees no distinction, they may say, "So that's how Christians act?"—not with admiration, but with disappointment. When we lash out at people, it destroys our testimony and defies what the Bible teaches us.

God's Word teaches us to work on ourselves and to be more Christ-like so that others can see Jesus shining in and through us. We are all a work in progress, so allow the Holy Spirit to continue helping you with your character. Gossip leads to destruction and can harm the person we are gossiping about (Ephesians 4:29). I am at fault here; when I was first saved, I did let slanderous talk come out of my mouth. What comes out of our mouths defiles us (Mark 7:15). Unwholesome talk is not the way of the Lord; it leads to a failure of character.

Allow God to take charge and build up your character so others will see Jesus living in us. Character is a vital aspect that makes us who we are in Christ. We are saints according to God's Word. Allow your character to be that of the person God created you to be.

Is our character in tune with God's character? How can we work on our character?

Prayer

'Loving Father, we ask You to help us to work on our character so people can see You shining in us, we ask You, Father, to guide us to the character You are and who You have called us to be in Jesus Christ's name. We pray. Amen.'

CONTROL OUR TONGUE

In many ways, our tongue can be a powerful weapon, whether for good or bad. What we say can make us strong or potentially do us more harm than we realize. I can recall a situation where my tongue got me into trouble. We have to be careful what we say to people. Our tongues can crush relationships, devour families, and tear us and others apart. In every situation, we must think before we speak. Be slow to speak (James 1:19). Allow the Holy Spirit to work in us so that our tongue does not get us into trouble.

James 3 speaks of taming the tongue. It is a small part of the body, but it makes great boasts (James 3:5). Learning to control our tongue helps us avoid saying things we might later regret. It allows us to communicate with wisdom and grace, which in turn strengthens and preserves our friendships. The tongue is also a fire, a world of evil among the parts of the body. It corrupts the whole body and sets the course of one's life on fire (James 3:5-6). Do not let your tongue create evil within you. Use it for God's glory.

With our tongue, we praise the Lord and Father, and with it, we curse human beings (James 3:9). How can we praise God and curse humans at the same time? Let God work in you so that your tongue will be used for His purpose and glory, not for harm. The tongue is a very powerful tool that can be used for good or bad. What will you use your tongue for?

How can you use your tongue for God's purpose and glory?

Prayer

'Dear Heaven Father, we come boldly before Your throne of grace and ask You to help us, use our tongues for Your purpose and glory. We ask You, Father, to help us control our tongues as we go into a broken world to share the good news and not to use our tongue to bring people down but to love them unconditionally as You love us (John 4:19) in Jesus Christ's name. We pray. Amen.'

INTRODUCTION CHURCH

Church should be a place where we are fed with the Word of God and where we make connections. However, has the church ever let you down? I think we can all relate to this feeling of disappointment. We need to put our faith in Jesus because people can let us down. After all, we are only human. If someone in the church does let us down, let's forgive them and move on—there is no sense in holding a grudge. Trust me, I have held grudges before, and it only hurts us in the end, making us the ones at fault.

The world can be an ugly place. I have been disappointed many times, even by the church—a place that should offer comfort. The church can sometimes be very judgmental. I have seen people in church praising Jesus, only to hang Him back on the cross by Monday. Unfortunately, that's just how the world operates sometimes. We need to be true to who we are.

When the church does let us down, we need to forgive, because it means our faith will grow stronger. My friend, let go of all the bitterness, hatred, and resentment, and give it to God. He will sustain you and lift you up. I have learned to put all of my hope and trust in Jesus. People, including those in the church, can let us down, but let's love them anyway. I have been let down by the church, and holding a grudge only hurts me.

Has the church let you down? How did you handle this?

Prayer

'Dear heavenly Father, when people do let us down, send Your comfort to us to show us Your perfect love that surpasses all understanding.'

CHURCH

Take heed therefore unto yourselves, and to all the flock, over the which the Holy Ghost hath made you overseers, to feed the church of God, which he hath purchased with his own blood. **Acts 20:26**

Praising God, and having favor with all the people. And the Lord added to the church daily such as should be saved. Acts 2:47

For as we have many members in one body, and all members have not the same office:

So, we, being many, are one body in Christ, and every member is one of another. **Romans 12:4-5**

Not forsaking the assembling of ourselves together, as the manner of some is; but exhorting one another: and so much the more, as ye see the day approaching. **Hebrews 10:25**

For where two or three are gathered together in my name, there am I in the midst of them. **Matthew 18:20**

For we are laborers together with God: ye are God's husbandry, ye are God's building. **1 Corinthians 3:9**

And I say also unto thee, That, thou art Peter, and upon this rock, I will build my church, and the gates of hell shall not prevail against it. **Matthew 16:18**

Now, therefore, ye are no more strangers and foreigners but fellow citizens with the saints, and of the household of God

And are built upon the foundation of the apostles and prophets, Jesus Christ himself being the chief cornerstone. **Ephesians 2:19-20**

And let the peace of God rule in your hearts, to the which also ye are called in one body; and be ye thankful. **Colossians 3:15**

For as the body is one, and hath many members, and all the members of that one body, being many, are one body: so also, is Christ. **1 Corinthians 12:12**

INTRODUCTION COMMITMENT TO GOD

Are we fully committed to God? Are we all in, or is there sin that we are still holding on to? I encourage you to let go and fully surrender and commit to God. I try my hardest to be fully committed to God at all times. We will fall short, and I understand that. If Jesus had fallen short, we would not be here. He was fully committed to the Father's will, to be the ransom for us to have everlasting life.

There are sacrifices involved in being fully committed to God. We need to surrender and submit to His will and allow the Holy Spirit to work on us. To be fully committed to God requires patience, letting go of sin, our egos, and the things that distract us and get in the way of God. One day we are hot; the next day we are cold. There should be no in-between—we should be hot at all times. Though we fall short, we should strive to be fully committed.

Make time with the Lord—pray, fast, and meditate on the Scriptures. There are blessings in being fully committed to God. He gives us wisdom, revelation, and restored relationships. It's a blessing and a privilege to serve the Lord. Let's work on ourselves to be fully committed.

How can we strive to be fully committed to God?

Prayer

'Dear Heavenly Father, work on us to be fully committed to you, show us ways to let go of distractions, to be more committed to You. I pray, Father, that we can let go of things and for Your Holy Spirit to work in us to be more committed, work on us to let go of pride, and to deny ourselves and pick up our cross and follow You in Jesus Christ's name. We pray. Amen.'

COMMITMENT TO GOD

Commit thy works unto the LORD, and thy thoughts shall be established. **Proverbs 16:3**

Let your heart therefore be perfect with the LORD our God, to walk in his statutes, and to keep his commandments, as at this day. **1 Kings 8:61**

Thou shalt therefore obey the voice of the LORD thy God, and do his commandments and his statutes, which I command thee this day. **Deuteronomy 27:10**

Into thine hand I commit my spirit: thou hast redeemed me, O LORD God of truth. **Psalm 31:5**

And let us not be weary in well doing: for in due season we shall reap if we faint not. **Galatians 6:9**

INTRODUCTION CONTENTMENT

Are we content with what God has given us? We have to be content in every situation. We should not covet our neighbor's possessions or want what we cannot have. I have to work on this—I have done this plenty of times. If we covet, it's a sin, and God wants us to work on this. He will give us what we need, not necessarily what we want.

The mission trip I went on in 2022 to Liberia, Africa, taught me what it really means to be content with what I have. Before the trip, I sometimes wanted more than what I had. The poverty in Liberia is horrible, and God sent me there to teach me a lesson. At times, I cursed my house, always wanting a big one. But the pastor I am connected with in Paynesville, Liberia, showed me a home where his brother lives—a 10x10 concrete shack. All he had was a bed and a few belongings—no kitchen, no electricity, no stove, nothing. Yet, he was very proud and joyful of his house. I was ashamed of myself. Here I was, wanting a better house, while there were people overseas who lived in extreme poverty, and some had no house at all.

I have all the things I need: a roof over my head, food, a car, and a job. The lessons the Holy Spirit taught me over there became the reasons why I will never speak ill of my house again. We are blessed in America, even though I know there are people struggling here, too. What I saw in Liberia broke me apart, and the mission trip changed my life forever. If a family is poor in Liberia, most of the children can't go to school. I hope I can go back and try to help them, and I am praying for God's will.

How can we help people who are less fortunate than us? I have been supporting the pastor I am connected with the little money I have. I know God will bless me, but I am not looking for a blessing—I am just helping him, and I do not expect anything in return. I love him with all of my heart. We have to be content in every situation; it could be worse. Most of the Africans make one dollar per day. There is no way we could survive here in the United States on a dollar per day. If we have a roof over our heads, we are blessed. If we have a job, we are blessed. If we have food, we are blessed. All the Lord wants us to do is be thankful and grateful for what we have and what we don't have.

I met a 12-year-old girl in Liberia who had no bed and slept outside. I wanted to take her home to the United States with me and give her a better life. The entire trip broke my heart. There are needs right here in America, too. An African lady brought her baby to the church; her baby had something wrong, but she could not afford to take the baby to the doctor. We prayed for a miracle healing. I don't know what became of our prayers for her and her baby, but I am continuing to pray for them. Just think of having a sick child and not being able to afford medical care, and the chance that your child could die—that would be devastating. We have government help here in the United States; I'm not sure about overseas. I am sure some nations have no help—you're just on your own.

I am beyond grateful that the Lord taught me to be content with everything I had when I went to Liberia. There are people out there who are not so fortunate. I am praying for supernatural funding to go back and help as much as I can so other people can eat, maybe get housing, help with agriculture, and teach their children about the Lord. I want to get support groups going for people who have addictions. It blew me away how joyful the nation of Liberia is despite the little they have. They gave the Lord all the glory, and the worship they performed in the church was glorious.

If we just help people a little, we can make a big difference. The Bible commands us to help if we can. How can we help people and get involved? I am praying for God's will to make a difference in this world, to make an impact for Jesus, for people to get saved, and to help those who are less fortunate than us. Let's be content with what we have.

Are we content with what we have, or do we want more than what we have? I am fully content with what God has given me.

Prayer

'Heavenly Father, please work in us to be content with what we have and to use us to help others and give them a helping hand.'

CONTENTMENT

But Godliness with contentment is great gain.

For we brought nothing into this world, and it is certain we can carry nothing out.

And having food and raiment, let us be therewith content.

But they that will be rich fall into temptation and a snare, and into many foolish and hurtful lusts, which drown men in destruction and perdition.

For the love of money is the root of all evil: which while some coveted after, they have erred from the faith, and pierced themselves through with many sorrows.

But thou, O man of God, flee these things; and follow after righteousness, Godliness, faith, love, patience, meekness. **1 Timothy 6:6-11**

Not that I speak in respect of want: for I have learned, in whatsoever state I am, therewith to be content.

I know both how to be abased, and I know how to abound: everywhere and in all things I am instructed both to be full and to be hungry, both to abound and to suffer need. **Philippians 4:11-12**

And the soldiers likewise demanded of him, saying, And what shall we do? And he said unto them, Do violence to no man, neither accuse any falsely; and be content with your wages. **Luke 3:14**

If they obey and serve him, they shall spend their days in prosperity, and their years in pleasures. **Job 36:11**

The young lions do lack, and suffer hunger: but they that seek the LORD shall not want any good thing. **Psalm 34:10**

Brethren, let every man, wherein he is called, therein abide with God. **1 Corinthians 7:24**

How much better is it to get wisdom than gold? and to get understanding rather than to be chosen than silver! **Proverbs 16:16**

Better is little with the fear of the LORD than great treasure and trouble therewith. **Proverbs 15:16**

Trust not in oppression, and become not vain in robbery: if riches increase, set not your heart upon them. **Psalm 62:10**

Better is the poor that walketh in his uprightness, than he that is perverse in his ways, though he be rich. **Proverbs 28:6**

A little that a righteous man hath is better than the riches of many wicked. **Psalm 37:16**

And he said unto his disciples, Therefore I say unto you, Take no thought for your life, what ye shall eat; neither for the body, what ye shall put on.

The life is more than meat, and the body is more than raiment.

Consider the ravens: for they neither sow nor reap; which neither have storehouse nor barn; and God feedeth them: how much more are ye better than the fowls? **Luke 12:22-24**

CHRIST MADE YOU WHO YOU ARE

God created you in His image and His likeness (Genesis 1:27). He created you for a purpose; you are unique, and no one is like you. Don't feel like you're never good enough—those thoughts are the enemy's way of getting into our minds to discourage us. When those thoughts arise, rebuke them. Satan has no place in your life; he wants us to fail. Remember, my friend, God created you to do marvelous things (John 14:12). Everything will work out for God's glory (Romans 8:28).

God's hand is on you. Never feel like you don't have potential or skill; the Lord has given you gifts to use for His glory. I remember a time when the enemy crept into my mind, and I believed a lie straight from the pit of hell. I was on the verge of giving up, convinced I wasn't good enough. But you are good enough. Jesus bought you at a price to do marvelous things for His glory and the Kingdom of Heaven.

God made you who you are for a special reason. He loves you and has set you apart (Ephesians 2:10). We are His workmanship, created in Christ Jesus for good works. The Holy Spirit will shine brightly in your walk with God. You can enable yourself to shrug off the negative thoughts of the enemy. My friend, God loves you, and He created you in His image. He made you perfectly (Jeremiah 1:5). He did not make a mistake. Never think that you are a mistake.

101

God loves you and has a purpose and a plan for your life.

How can we resist the enemy, so we know what God's plan is for us?

Prayer

'Heavenly Father, we know that You created us to be like You. Please, Father, send us Your love to know that You made us in Your image to do good works, so that people will see You in us in Jesus Christ's name. We pray. Amen.'

INTRODUCTION DISCIPLESHIP

We are called to make disciples, wherever we go the Holy Spirit will lead us, to the people he wants us to minister to, and to making disciples is very rewarding. We get to encourage people, share the gospel, teach them, guide them, and help them on their walk and journey with God. Jesus is very happy that we take the time to build up the people, he leads us to the main part of the gospel is making disciples, which is our number one mission, the great commission.

How has God used you to make disciples in your community, and what was the outcome of the people that the Lord used you to lead?

Prayer

'Heavenly Father, lead us to the people in our community whom You want us to disciple. Please, God, send us more people to make disciples and build up Your kingdom and save people from going to hell in the last days.'

DISCIPLESHIP

And he said to them all, if any man will come after me, let him deny himself, and take up his cross daily, and follow me.

For whosoever will save his life shall lose it: but whosoever will lose his life for my sake, the same shall save it.

For what is a man advantaged, if he gains the whole world, and loses himself, or be cast away? **Luke 9:23-25**

And when he had called the people unto him with his disciples also, he said unto them, Whosoever, will come after me, let him deny himself, and take up his cross, and follow me. **Mark 8:34**

And whosoever doth not bear his cross, and come after me, cannot be my disciple. **Luke 14:26-27**

So likewise, whosoever he be of you that forsaketh not all that he hath, he cannot be my disciple. **Luke 14:33**

Then said Jesus to those Jews who believed in him, If ye continue in my word, then are ye my disciples indeed;

And ye shall know the truth, and the truth shall make you free. **John 8:31-32**

A new commandment I give unto you, That ye love one another; as

I have loved you, that ye also love one another.

By this shall all men know that ye are my disciples if ye have love one to another. **John 13:34-35**

Then said Jesus unto his disciples, If any man will come after me, let him deny himself, and take up his cross, and follow me. **Matthew 16:24**

Go ye therefore, and teach all nations, baptizing them in the name of the Father, and of the Son, and of the Holy Ghost:

Teaching them to observe all things whatsoever I have commanded you: and, lo, I am with you always, even unto the end of the world. Amen. **Matthew 28:19-20**

This beginning of miracles did Jesus in Cana of Galilee and manifested forth his glory, and his disciples believed in him. **John 2:11**

Let your light so shine before men, that they may see your good works, and glorify your Father which is in heaven. **Matthew 5:16**

The disciple is not above his master: but everyone that is perfect shall be his master. **Luke 6:40**

Herein is my Father glorified, that ye bear much fruit; so shall ye be my disciples. **John 15:8**

INTRODUCTION DISCERNMENT

Do you have discernment? Do you want it? All you have to do is ask God for it, and He will give it to you. Discernment is the ability to distinguish between truth and error, right and wrong. The Lord has given my dad and me supernatural discernment—the ability to see right through people and discern if they are good or bad, and to perceive truths about them.

Many times, I have discerned certain truths about people or teachers of the Bible. God will show us who to hang out with and who to avoid. All we have to do is pray for discernment, and He will give it to us. Some people have more discernment than others. One of my biggest gifts is discernment—the ability to look into people or situations and determine if I need to make a change. The Lord often gives me a dream and then puts me on the right path.

The Lord may also use us to discern for others. For example, if we dream about people, it could be a hint from the Holy Spirit to pray for them.

Do you have discernment of how the lord used you to operate in this gift?

Prayer

'Dear heavenly Father, I pray for people to be more discerning, especially in the last days, to sue us to help other believers operate in this gift in Jesus' name. We pray. Amen.'

DISCERNMENT

Give therefore thy servant an understanding heart to judge thy people, that I may discern between good and bad: for who is able to judge this thy so great a people? **1 Kings 3:9**

But strong meat belongeth to them that are of full age, even those who by reason of use have their senses exercised to discern both good and evil. **Hebrews 5:14**

Who is wise, and he shall understand these things? prudent, and he shall know them? for the ways of the LORD are right, and the just shall walk in them: but the transgressors shall fall therein. **Hosea 14:9**

But the natural man receiveth not the things of the Spirit of God: for they are foolishness unto him: neither can he know them, because they are spiritually discerned. **1 Corinthians 2:14**

For God is not the author of confusion, but of peace, as in all churches of the saints. **1 Corinthians 14:33**

Behold, I send you forth as sheep in the midst of wolves: be ye therefore wise as serpents, and harmless as doves. **Matthew 10:16**

And be not conformed to this world: but be ye transformed by the renewing of your mind, that ye may prove what is that good, and acceptable, and perfect, will of God. **Romans 12:2**

If any of you lack wisdom, let him ask of God, that giveth to all men liberally, and upbraideth not; and it shall be given him. **James 1:5**

To another the working of miracles; to another prophecy; to another discerning of spirits; to another divers kinds of tongues; to another the interpretation of tongues. **1 Corinthians 12:10**

INTRODUCTION DEPRESSION

Depression is incredibly difficult, and my heart goes out to you. I pray that the Lord lifts you out of this darkness and brings people into your life who will walk alongside you with love, support, and understanding. The Lord is with you, and He will hold you by the hand and tell you everything will turn out to be ok. I hope that Jesus will heal you of this.

Has depression been a struggle for you?

Prayer

'Dear heavenly Father, I pray for those who are depressed that you help them through this, Lord. Whoever is reading this who is depressed, I pray that You can heal them of their depression and break this in Jesus Christ's name. I pray. Amen.'

DEPRESSION

Come unto me, all ye that labor and are heavy laden, and I will give you rest.

Take my yoke upon you, and learn of me; for I am meek and lowly in heart: and ye shall find rest unto your souls.

For my yoke is easy, and my burden is light. **Matthew 11:28-30**

Hear me speedily, O LORD: my spirit faileth: hide not thy face from me, lest I be like unto them that go down into the pit. **Psalm 143:7**

When thou saidst, Seek ye my face; my heart said unto thee, Thy face, LORD, will I seek. **Psalm 27:8**

The LORD also will be a refuge for the oppressed, a refuge in times of trouble. **Psalm 9:9**

The LORD is nigh unto them that are of a broken heart; and saveth such as be of a contrite spirit. **Psalms 34:18**

For I the LORD thy God will hold thy right hand, saying unto thee, Fear not; I will help thee. **Isaiah 41:13**

And kings shall be thy nursing fathers, and their queens thy nursing mothers: they shall bow down to thee with their face toward the earth, and lick up the dust of thy feet and thou shalt know that I am the LORD: for they shall not be ashamed that wait for me. **Isaiah 49:23**

Blessed be God, even the Father of our Lord Jesus Christ, the Father of mercies, and the God of all comfort;

Who comforteth us in all our tribulation, that we may be able to comfort them which are in any trouble, by the comfort wherewith we ourselves are comforted of God. **2 Corinthians 1:3-4**

The steps of a good man are ordered by the LORD: and he delighteth in his way.

Though he falls, he shall not be utterly cast down: for the LORD upholdeth him with his hand. **Psalm 37:23-24**

For his anger endureth but a moment; in his favor is life: weeping may endure for a night, but joy cometh in the morning. **Psalm 30:5**

Nevertheless, God, that comforteth those that are cast down, comforted us by the coming of Titus. **2 Corinthians 7:6**

For thou art my lamp, O LORD: and the LORD will lighten my darkness. **2 Samuel 22:29**

Why art thou cast down, O my soul? and why art thou disquieted in me? hope thou in God: for I shall yet praise him for the help of his countenance. **Psalm 42:5**

INTRODUCTION EVANGELISM

We should strive to evangelize the gospel. People share the gospel in different ways; there is no wrong or right way to share it. However, there are better ways. When I gave my life back to the Lord, I was very headstrong. I used to thump people in the head with the Bible, and that was not the right approach. It doesn't reflect love and can cause us to come across as judgmental.

God reminds us to stay humble and let the Holy Spirit do the talking, rather than us doing the speaking. God tells us in His Word to preach the Word (2 Timothy 4:2 KJV). However, He does not say to evangelize out of arrogance or judgment—that is God's job, not ours. I have experienced this myself, and it only set me back rather than forward. It drives people further from God when we come across as judgmental.

We should aim to bring people closer to God. Think of better ways to share your faith and the gospel. Share it out of love, because love covers a multitude of sins (1 Peter 4:8 KJV). If we love people for who they are, we will reach more people, and the Great Commission will have better results (Matthew 28:16-20 KJV).

I encourage you to step out of your comfort zone and let God use you to help save those who are lost (Proverbs 11:30 KJV).

Evangelizing is very important, and we should strive to do it effectively. Be leaders in your community. Pastors have many responsibilities, and it is our job to help them. I encourage you to pray for your pastors daily and for our leaders in the world. Pray for our governments to change. Ask your pastor how you can help serve; they might put you on a team someday to help them evangelize in the community.

How can you share your faith today to lead others to the Lord

(Revelation 12:11 KJV)? The results could be amazing, and you can share these results with your church.

How do you Evangelize in your community? Have you had some amazing results?

Prayer

'Heavenly Father, gracious Lord, use us in our community to Evangelize Your Word, to set the captives free, heal the sick, and proclaim Your Word at all costs. Please, Father, send us people to mentor and save.

EVANGELISM

And he said unto them, Go ye into all the world, and preach the gospel to every creature. **Mark 16:15**

But watch thou in all things, endure afflictions, do the work of an evangelist, make full proof of thy ministry. **2 Timothy 4:5**

For so hath the Lord commanded us, saying, I have set thee to be a light of the Gentiles, that thou shouldest be for salvation unto the ends of the earth. **Acts 13:47**

The Spirit of the Lord is upon me because he hath anointed me to preach the gospel to the poor; he hath sent me to heal the brokenhearted, to preach deliverance to the captives, and recovering of sight to the blind, to set at liberty them that are bruised. **Luke 4:18**

Preach the word; be instant in season, out of season; reprove, rebuke, exhort with all long-suffering and doctrine. **2 Timothy 4:2**

And in that day shall ye say, Praise the LORD, call upon his name, declare his doings among the people, make mention that his name is exalted. **Isaiah 12:4**

But speak thou the things which become sound doctrine. **Titus 2:1**

Then saith he unto his disciples, The harvest truly is plenteous, but the laborers are few.

Pray ye, therefore, the Lord of the harvest, that he will send forth laborers into his harvest. **Matthew 9:37-38**

Also, I heard the voice of the Lord, saying, Whom shall I send, and who will go for us? Then said I, Here am I; send me. **Isaiah 6:8**

For the Son of man is come to seek and to save that which was lost. **Luke 19:10**

Now then we are ambassadors for Christ, as though God did beseech you by us: we pray you in Christ's stead, be ye reconciled to God. 2 **Corinthians 5:20**

The fruit of the righteous is a tree of life, and he that winneth souls is wise. **Proverbs 11:30**

That the communication of thy faith may become effectual by the acknowledging of every good thing which is in you in Christ Jesus. **Philemon 6**

For though I preach the gospel, I have nothing to glory of for necessity is laid upon me; yea, woe is unto me, if I preach not the gospel! 1 **Corinthians 9:16**

But it is good for me to draw near to God: I have put my trust in the

Lord GOD, that I may declare all thy works. **Psalm 73:28**

How then shall they call on him in whom they have not believed? and how shall they believe in him of whom they have not heard? and how shall they hear without a preacher? **Romans 10:14**

But none of these things move me, neither count I my life dear unto myself, so that I might finish my course with joy, and the ministry, which I have received of the Lord Jesus, to testify the gospel of the grace of God. **Acts 20:24**

And some have compassion, making a difference:

And others save with fear, pulling them out of the fire; hating even the garment spotted by the flesh.

Now unto him that is able to keep you from falling, and to present you faultless before the presence of his glory with exceeding joy,

To the only wise God our Saviour, be glory and majesty, dominion and power, both now and ever. Amen. **Jude 22-25**

INTRODUCTION ETERNAL LIFE

Eternal life is what we long for. It is forever and ever. Not long ago, I was heading down a road that was leading to my destruction. God intervened, washed me clean, and gave me a new path. Eternal life is a promise for those who are in Christ. Those who are not in Christ are headed for hell.

I preach that heaven is real and glorious, and hell is hot—it is no place to go. If you still have breath, there is hope. If people die without Jesus, they are going to hell. I write this to encourage you to remain in Christ and to be a light to others, saving them from the depths of hell (Jude 17-25 KJV). Our job is to share our testimony and lead others to eternal life.

I encourage you to write agape letters of love to be left behind for the survivors of the rapture during the tribulation. Those who are not in Christ will be left behind. In these letters, share your faith and tell people how to receive Jesus as their Lord and Savior. Explain that they have to invite Jesus into their hearts to be saved. This will greatly impact the Kingdom of God during the tribulation, even though the Holy Spirit will be gone. Share your love for Christ in these letters so that the people in the tribulation have something to fall back on.

I have written letters to be left behind for people during that time, to give them hope. You never know what kind of impact these letters will have. Leave them in your home. Write sermon notes to be left behind. Document your testimony, sharing how God changed your life, how the Holy Spirit has been present, and how you invited Jesus into your heart to be the Lord of your life. Explain how you repented of your sins and turned away from them, and how God gave you grace when you did not deserve it.

The survivors of the rapture are counting on us for eternal life.

How has gaining eternal life changed your inside, and for the Holy Spirit's presence in your life been evident in the forgiveness of sins?

Prayer

'Dear Heavenly Father, send Your holy Spirit down to us to lead others and use us to give people eternal life and speak life into the lost.'

ETERNAL LIFE

Verily, verily, I say unto you, He that heareth my word, and believeth on him that sent me, hath everlasting life, and shall not come into condemnation; but is passed from death unto life. **John 5:24**

For the wages of sin is death, but the gift of God is eternal life through Jesus Christ our Lord. **Romans 6:23**

Jesus said unto her, I am the resurrection, and the life: he that believeth in me, though he were dead, yet shall he live:

And whosoever liveth and believeth in me shall never die. Believest thou this? **John 11:25-26**

And I give unto them eternal life, and they shall never perish, neither shall any man pluck them out of my hand.

My Father, which gave them me, is greater than all; and no man is able to pluck them out of my Father's hand.

I and my Father are one. **John 10:28-30**

For whoso findeth me findeth life, and shall obtain favor of the LORD. Proverbs 8:35

And the world passeth away, and the lust thereof: but he that doeth the will of God abideth forever. **1 John 2:17**

And this is the record, that God hath given to us eternal life, and this life is in his Son. **1 John 5:11**

These things have I written unto you that believe on the name of the Son of God; that ye may know that ye have eternal life and that ye may believe in the name of the Son of God. **1 John 5:13**

And this is life eternal, that they might know thee the only true God, and Jesus Christ, whom thou hast sent. **John 17:3**

He that believeth on the Son hath everlasting life: and he that believeth not the Son shall not see life, but the wrath of God abideth on him. **John 3:36**

Fight the good fight of faith, lay hold on eternal life, whereunto thou art also called, and hast professed a good profession before many witnesses. **1 Timothy 6:12**

But whosoever drinketh of the water that I shall give him shall never thirst; but the water that I shall give him shall be in him a well of water springing up into everlasting life. **John 4:14**

For he that soweth to his flesh shall of the flesh reap corruption; but he that soweth to the Spirit shall of the Spirit reap life everlasting. **Galatians 6:8**

Enter ye in at the strait gate: for wide is the gate, and broad is the way, that leadeth to destruction, and many there be which go in thereat:

Because strait is the gate, and narrow is the way, which leadeth unto life, and few there be that find it. **Matthew 7:13-14**

And this is the will of him that sent me, that every one which seeth the Son, and believeth on him, may have everlasting life: and I will raise him up at the last day. **John 6:40**

And these shall go away into everlasting punishment: but the righteous into life eternal. **Matthew 25:46**

INTRODUCTION FORGIVENESS

It is not easy to ask for forgiveness for the wrongs we do to people. I recall a situation at my job where I lashed out, and God was tugging at my heart to ask for forgiveness. It was hard to admit I was in the wrong. However, if we humble ourselves and ask for forgiveness, God forgives us. If we hold onto resentment and unforgiveness, we will not progress in our ministry with the Lord.

I have had to ask people to forgive me many times, and it shows that we are not like the world. Let's work out our problems with people and humble ourselves. It could bring a broken relationship into restoration. Unforgiveness is a dark cloud always hovering over us; it is a tool of Satan.

My friend, God wants to teach us to always forgive others because Jesus forgave us by going to the cross to die for our sins. If people lash out or say things they don't like, just smile and walk away.

When did you have to forgive someone even though you didn't want to? Was it hard to forgive?

Prayer

'Loving Father, please help us to forgive others even when we don't want to. Please keep Your love in us to forgive people. Amen.'

FORGIVENESS

And be ye kind one to another, tenderhearted, forgiving one another, even as God for Christ's sake hath forgiven you. **Ephesians 4:32**

And when ye stand praying, forgive, if ye have ought against any: that your Father also which is in heaven may forgive you your trespasses. **Mark 11:25**

If we confess our sins, he is faithful and just to forgive us our sins, and to cleanse us from all unrighteousness. **1 John 1:9**

Then came Peter to him, and said, Lord, how oft shall my brother sin against me, and I forgive him? till seven times?

Jesus saith unto him, I say not unto thee, Until seven times: but, Until seventy times seven. **Matthew 18:21-22**

For if ye forgive men their trespasses, your heavenly Father will also forgive you:

But if ye forgive not men their trespasses, neither will your Father forgive your trespasses. **Matthew 6:14-15**

For bearing one another, and forgiving one another, if any man has a quarrel against any: even as Christ forgave you, so also do ye.

Colossians 3:13

And when they have come to the place, which is called Calvary, there they crucified him, and the malefactors, one on the right hand, and the other on the left.

Then said Jesus, Father, forgive them; for they know not what they do. And they parted his raiment and cast lots. **Luke 23:33-34**

To the Lord, our God belongs mercies and forgiveness, though we have rebelled against him. **Daniel 9:9**

I acknowledge my sin unto thee, and mine iniquity have I not hid. I said, I will confess my transgressions unto the LORD, and thou forgavest the iniquity of my sin. **Psalm 32:5**

Take heed to yourselves: If thy brother trespass against thee, rebuke him; and if he repent, forgive him.

And if he trespass against thee seven times in a day, and seven times in a day turn again to thee, saying, I repent; thou shalt forgive him. **Luke 17:3-4**

As far as the east is from the west, so far hath he removed our transgressions from us. **Psalm 103:12**

Who hath delivered us from the power of darkness, and hath translated us into the kingdom of his dear Son:

In whom we have redemption through his blood, even the forgiveness of sins. **Colossians 1:13-14**

INTRODUCTION FAITH

We have to have faith that God will do the impossible. Trust Him; He will give you ultimate faith. Have faith to do what God has called you to do because faith without works is dead. Having faith as tiny as a mustard seed can sprout and turn into big things. Have faith in the small things that we do for the Lord, and He will give you bigger tasks to accomplish.

I remember when I was just five years old, helping my grandmother plant pumpkin seeds in her garden. We worked hard to get it done, and after we were finished, I asked her if I could have one of her pumpkin seeds to take home and plant in my mother's garden. I took the seed, put it in my hand, and my grandmother gave me a ride home. My mother had just finished planting her garden, and when I showed her the seed and asked if I could plant it, she said no, as she had just completed the garden and felt it wouldn't grow. I started crying and kicking my feet. Finally, she relented and let me plant it in the corner. I dug up the dirt with my little shovel, planted the seed, and watered it. When I was done, I prayed and asked God to help grow this seed. That one little seed I planted eventually took over her entire garden; she had no produce that year, just a bunch of pumpkins. My mother was amazed. I had faith in that one little seed, and God honored it.

All we need is faith, and then the Holy Spirit will work in the supernatural. I started with small things, and God gave me bigger assignments. I became an ordained minister in my community and went on a mission trip to Liberia, Africa. It was a trip to store up treasures in heaven. God used me to save an African lady who was on the edge of suicide; I prayed for her, and the Holy Spirit used me to revive her. I preached to thousands of Africans, and many came to the Lord through my testimony. I will eventually go back when the time is right. I also ministered to the children of Africa—they are the future of Liberia.

What an amazing journey God put me on! I had faith that God was going to use me mightily, and He did. I write articles for our town newspaper. I always pray over them first and pray afterward that the people in this community who read the articles will be encouraged and that God will use my writings to speak life into my community and to save those who are lost.

Have faith, my friend. God will use you right where you are.

How has your faith in the Lord helped you in your ministry and the battles we often go through to rely on the lord in times of need?

Prayer

'Heavenly Father, please give us faith in You to carry on the works that You have given us. Please use us for Your glory.'

FAITH

And all things, whatsoever ye shall ask in prayer, believing, ye shall receive. **Matthew 21:22**

For we walk by faith, not by sight. **2 Corinthians 5:7**

So then faith cometh by hearing and hearing by the word of God. **Romans 10:17**

Now faith is the substance of things hoped for, the evidence of things not seen. **Hebrews 11:1**

And Jesus said unto them, Because of your unbelief: for verily I say unto you, If ye have faith as a grain of mustard seed, ye shall say unto this mountain, Remove hence to yonder place; and it shall remove, and nothing shall be impossible unto you. **Matthew 17:20**

That your faith should not stand in the wisdom of men, but in the power of God. **1 Corinthians 2:5**

I have fought a good fight, I have finished my course, I have kept the faith. **2 Timothy 4:7**

Behold, his soul which is lifted up is not upright in him: but the just shall live by his faith. **Habakkuk 2:4**

I am crucified with Christ: nevertheless, I live; yet not I, but Christ liveth in me: and the life which I now live in the flesh I live by the faith of the Son of God, who loved me and gave himself for me. **Galatians 2:20**

For ye are all the children of God by faith in Christ Jesus. **Galatians 3:26**

As ye have therefore received Christ Jesus the Lord, so walk ye in him:

Rooted and built up in him, and established in the faith, as ye have been taught, abounding therein with thanksgiving. **Colossians 2:6-7**

And Jesus answering saith unto them, Have faith in God.

For verily I say unto you, That whosoever shall say unto this mountain, Be thou removed, and be thou cast into the sea; and shall not doubt in his heart, but shall believe that those things which he saith shall come to pass; he shall have whatsoever he saith. **Mark 11:22-23**

Even so, faith, if it hath not worked, is dead, being alone. **James 2:17**

INTRODUCTION FALSE PROPHETS

Today, many false prophets speak only what people want to hear, not what they need to hear. In the Old Testament, false prophets were put to death. When someone has a Word from God to share with you, always test the spirits, pray, and ask God; the Holy Spirit will show you whether the word came from God or not. I have had people speak into my life. Some words have been true, some have been misleading. Always seek the Lord in everything. There are a lot of voices now, and we have to be able to discern if it is God's voice.

Have you had a time in your life when the voice was misleading or true? We have to discern if it is the Lord.

Prayer

'Dear Heavenly Father, there are a lot of voices out there that can be misleading. I pray, Father, for this generation that people are not led astray. In Jesus' name, Amen.'

FALSE PROPHETS

Beloved, believe not every spirit, but try the spirits whether they are of God: because many false prophets are gone out into the world. **1 John 4:1**

Beware of false prophets, which come to you in sheep's clothing, but inwardly they are ravening wolves. **Matthew 7:15**

But there were false prophets also among the people, even as there shall be false teachers among you, who privily shall bring in damnable heresies, even denying the Lord that bought them and bring upon themselves swift destruction. **2 Peter 2:1**

For there shall arise false Christs and false prophets, and shall shew great signs and wonders; insomuch that, if it were possible, they shall deceive the very elect. **Matthew 24:24**

For they that are such serve, not our Lord Jesus Christ, but their own belly; and by good words and fair speeches deceive the hearts of the simple. **Romans 16:18**

But the prophet, which shall presume to speak a word in my name, which I have not commanded him to speak, or that shall speak in the name of other Gods, even that prophet shall die.

And if thou say in thine heart, How shall we know the word which the LORD hath not spoken?

When a prophet speaketh in the name of the LORD, if the thing follows not, nor come to pass, that is the thing which the LORD hath not spoken, but the prophet hath spoken it presumptuously: thou shalt not be afraid of him. **Deuteronomy 18:20-22**

For such are false apostles, deceitful workers, transforming themselves into the apostles of Christ. And no marvel; for Satan himself is transformed into an angel of light.

Therefore, it is no great thing if his ministers also be transformed as the ministers of righteousness; whose end shall be according to their works. **2 Corinthians 11:13-15**

And the devil that deceived them was cast into the lake of fire and brimstone, where the beast and the false prophet are, and shall be tormented day and night forever and ever. **Revelation 20:10**

And mine hand shall be upon the prophets that see vanity, and that divine lies: they shall not be in the assembly of my people, neither shall they be written in the writing of the house of Israel, neither shall they enter into the land of Israel; and ye shall know that I am the Lord GOD. **Ezekiel 13:9**

Then the LORD said unto me, The prophets prophesy lies in my name: I sent them not, neither have I commanded them, neither spake unto them: they prophesy unto you a false vision and divination, and a thing of naught, and the deceit of their heart. **Jeremiah 14:14**

Woe unto you, when all men shall speak well of you! for so did their fathers to the false prophets. **Luke 6:26**

Thus, saith the LORD of hosts, Hearken not unto the words of the prophets that prophesy unto you: they make you vain: they speak a vision of their own heart, and not out of the mouth of the LORD.

They say still unto them that despise me, The LORD hath said, Ye shall have peace; and they say unto every one that walketh after the imagination of his own heart, No evil shall come upon you. **Jeremiah 23:16-17**

Then said the prophet Jeremiah unto Hananiah the prophet, Hear now, Hananiah; The LORD hath not sent thee; but thou makest this person to trust in a lie. **Jeremiah 28:15**

And her prophets have daubed them with untempered mortar, seeing vanity, and divining lies unto them, saying, Thus, saith the Lord GOD, when the LORD hath not spoken. **Ezekiel 22:28**

And when they had gone through the isle unto Paphos, they found a certain sorcerer, a false prophet, a Jew, whose name was Bar-Jesus. **Acts 13:6**

And the beast was taken, and with him the false prophet that wrought miracles before him, with which he deceived them that had received the mark of the beast, and them that worshipped his image. These both were cast alive into a lake of fire burning with brimstone. **Revelation 19:20**

A wonderful and horrible thing is committed in the land;

The prophets prophesy falsely, and the priests bear rule by their means, and my people love to have it so: and what will ye do at the end thereof? **Jeremiah 5:30-31**

INTRODUCTION FALSE TEACHERS

Some teachers today cater only to itching ears, telling people what they want to hear. We must be bold in rebuking false teachers and standing firm in the truth. Pray that the Holy Spirit will convict them. In the last few days, we have had to be careful who we listen to. About four years ago, I was going to almost everyone to get answers. God then spoke to me, only to be attentive to my voice and my commands. Listen to those whom I have appointed. False teachers lead us astray. Wondering in the fields with misunderstanding and misconception, I have been down this road before listening to false teachers. I once heard that if you don't speak in tongues, you will not be raptured. I could not agree with that. That is a false teaching, it's heresy. You must check your bible out for yourself on all teachings. There is a lot of teaching out there, and sometimes they tell you only what they want you to hear. The Word of God will not return void.

In the past two years, I have narrowed down who I listen to because God told me so. The Bible warns against false teachers. I pray that you will be able to discern what is sound doctrine and what is not.

Have you ever been led astray by false teaching? How did you bounce back from that?

Prayer

'Dear Heavenly Father, I pray that we can be able to discern what is right and wrong when it comes to teaching. I pray, Father, that the people reading this book have sound teaching. If not, I pray that You can lead them to the right teaching. We must be careful who we listen to in the last days. In Jesus' name, Amen.'

FALSE TEACHERS

For the time will come when they will not endure sound doctrine; but after their own lusts shall they heap to themselves teachers, having itching ears;

And they shall turn away their ears from the truth and shall be turned unto fables. **2 Timothy 4:3-4**

If any man teaches otherwise and consents not to wholesome words, even the words of our Lord Jesus Christ, and to the doctrine which is according to Godliness;

He is proud, knowing nothing, but doting about questions and strifes of words, whereof cometh envy, strife, railings, evil surmisings, perverse disputings of men of corrupt minds, and destitute of the truth, supposing that gain is Godliness: from such withdraw thyself. **1 Timothy 6:3-5**

For there are certain men crept in unawares, who were before of old ordained to this condemnation, ungodly men, turning the grace of our God into lasciviousness, and denying the only Lord God, and our Lord Jesus Christ. **Jude 4**

And have no fellowship with the unfruitful works of darkness, but rather reprove them. **Ephesians 5:11**

These things have I written unto you concerning them that seduce you.

But the anointing which ye have received of him abideth in you, and ye need not that any man teach you: but as the same anointing teacheth you of all things, and is truth, and is no lie, and even as it hath taught you, ye shall abide in him. **1 John 2:26-27**

But evil men and seducers shall wax worse and worse, deceiving, and being deceived. **2 Timothy 3:11**

Now I beseech you, brethren, mark them which cause divisions and offenses contrary to the doctrine which ye have learned; and avoid them.

For they that are such serve, not our Lord Jesus Christ, but their own belly; and by good words and fair speeches deceive the hearts of the simple. **Romans 16:17-18**

Beware lest any man spoil you through philosophy and vain deceit, after the tradition of men, after the rudiments of the world, and not after Christ. **Colossians 2:8**

But the tongue can no man tame; it is an unruly evil, full of deadly poison. **James 3:1**

O Timothy, keep that which is committed to thy trust, avoiding profane and vain babblings, and oppositions of science falsely so-called:

Which some professing have erred concerning the faith. Grace be with thee. Amen. **1 Timothy 6:20-21**

Holding fast the faithful word as he hath been taught, that he may be able by sound doctrine both to exhort and to convince the gainsayers.

For there are many unruly and vain talkers and deceivers, especially they of the circumcision:

Whose mouths must be stopped, who subvert whole houses, teaching things which they ought not, for filthy lucre's sake. **Titus 1:9-11**

Knowing this first, that no prophecy of the scripture is of any private interpretation.

For the prophecy came not in old time by the will of man: but holy men of God spake as they were moved by the Holy Ghost. **2 Peter 1:20-21**

As I besought thee to abide still at Ephesus, when I went into Macedonia, that thou mightest charge some that they teach no other doctrine. **1 Timothy 1:3**

For whoremongers, for them that defile themselves with mankind, for menstealers, for liars, for perjured persons, and if there be any other thing that is contrary to sound doctrine. **1 Timothy 1:10**

That we henceforth are no more children, tossed to and fro, and carried about with every wind of doctrine, by the sleight of men, and cunning craftiness, whereby they lie in wait to deceive;

But speaking the truth in love may grow up into him in all things, which is the head, even Christ:

From whom the whole body fitly joined together and compacted by that which every joint supplieth, according to the effectual working in the measure of every part, maketh increase of the body unto the edifying of itself in love. **Ephesians 4:14-16**

INTRODUCTION FAVOR

God favors His children; we are His prized possession. He showed us favor by going to the cross. How has God favored you in your life? He has favored me many times. All we have to do to be favored is remain in Him and in His Word. The favor of God is His abundant love for us. The Lord gives us what we need, and sometimes He gives us more than we need—that, my friend, is a blessing and favor.

We can also show favor to others by helping them with their needs and by discipling them in God's Word. The favor of God blesses His people for being obedient and faithful. Moses was favored by God to have Aaron speak for him. Joseph was favored by God; although he was sold by his brothers and imprisoned, he eventually became second in command in Egypt. The favor of God was upon him. There are many stories in the Bible that talk about favor. We sometimes don't see favor right away, but it eventually comes. Joseph did not see favor until years later, after being imprisoned and then released. He became second in command in Egypt and saved the nation during a famine. The favor of God was upon him.

So many times, we have received favor from the Lord. We are His people, chosen to do good works. The more we do, the more we are favored by God. We have to be faithful in the small beginnings; if we remain faithful in those, the Lord will favor us and give us bigger things to do for Him. He wants us to be loyal to Him. I started out small and eventually went on a mission trip to Africa. The Lord favored me by allowing me to go and share my testimony with thousands of people. The village I visited was inspired by my testimony and what God did for me. He favored me by putting my burdens upon Him and transforming me in a matter of seconds.

There are many favors the Lord gives us. We have to be obedient to Him, or some of the favor of the Lord may be withheld unless we repent and turn away. My friend, remain in Christ, and the favor of the Holy Spirit will be upon you.

How did the Lord give you favor in your life and ministry? Did you thank Him for the things He has done for us?

Prayer

'Dear heavenly Father, we thank You for the favor that You give us even when we don't deserve it. Your favor that is upon us gives us Joy to share with people, how You are working in our life, please continue to do good work in us.'

FAVOR

For his anger endureth but a moment; in his favor is life: weeping may endure for a night, but joy cometh in the morning. **Psalm 30:5**

For thou, LORD, wilt bless the righteous; with favor wilt, thou compass him as with a shield. **Psalm 5:12**

For the LORD God is a sun and shield: the LORD will give grace and glory: no good thing will he withhold from them that walk uprightly. **Psalm 84:11**

But Noah found grace in the eyes of the LORD. **Genesis 6:8**

And said, My LORD, if now I have found favor in thy sight, pass not away, I pray thee, from thy servant. **Genesis 18:3**

And Jesus increased in wisdom and stature, and in favor with God and man. **Luke 2:52**

And Joseph found grace in his sight, and he served him: and he made him overseer over his house, and all that he had he put into his hand. **Genesis 39:4**

Whoso findeth a wife findeth a good thing, and obtaineth favor of the LORD. **Proverbs 18:22**

And Laban said unto him, I pray thee, if I have found favor in thine eyes, tarry: for I have learned by experience that the LORD hath blessed me for thy sake. **Genesis 30:27**

But the LORD was with Joseph and showed him mercy, and gave him favor in the sight of the keeper of the prison. **Genesis 39:21**

And the LORD gave the people favor in the sight of the Egyptians. Moreover, the man Moses was very great in the land of Egypt, in the sight of Pharaoh's servants, and in the sight of the people. **Exodus 11:3**

For it was of the LORD to harden their hearts, that they should come against Israel in battle, that he might destroy them utterly, and that they might have no favor, but that he might destroy them, as the LORD commanded Moses. **Joshua 11:20**

And the child Samuel grew on and was in favor both with the LORD and also with men. **1 Samuel 2:26**

Let them shout for joy, and be glad, that favor my righteous cause: yea, let them say continually, Let the LORD be magnified, which hath pleasure in the prosperity of his servant. **Psalm 35:27**

For they got not the land in possession by their own sword, neither did their own arm save them: but thy right hand, and thine arm, and the light of thy countenance, because thou hadst a favor unto them. **Psalms 44:3**

A good man sheweth favor, and lendeth: he will guide his affairs with discretion. **Psalm 112:5**

So shalt thou find favor and good understanding in the sight of God and man. **Proverbs 3:4**

For whoso findeth me findeth life, and shall obtain favor of the LORD. **Proverbs 8;35**

He that diligently seeketh good procureth favor: but he that seeketh mischief, it shall come unto him. **Proverbs 11:27**

INTRODUCTION FOLLOWING JESUS

Following Jesus comes with a cost. When I gave my life back to the Lord, I lost some friends along the way. But I've come to understand that not everyone can walk with you on the path of faith. Have you ever experienced a moment when following Jesus cost you something? Maybe it was rejection, ridicule, or even being laughed at. You're not alone—many of us have faced these trials, but the reward of walking with Him is far greater than anything we leave behind. That's okay; it will happen. The disciples were killed for their faith in Christ, except John, who was exiled to the island of Patmos. That is where he had the visions and wrote the book of Revelation.

I encourage you to remain steadfast in the Lord's Word. There will be a cost to follow Jesus, and it can come in many ways, shapes, and forms. Let's stand firm until the end. I gave up drugs and alcohol to follow Jesus. If you're still struggling with that, I want to encourage you to let go of it. Jesus can help you with anything. Giving up drugs and alcohol was the best decision I have ever made. There are rewards stored up in heaven for following Jesus at all costs.

If we follow Jesus, we will be persecuted—that's evident. The Bible says that we will be tempted by Satan. Don't give in. Follow Jesus and rebuke the voice of the enemy. He just wants to keep us from following Jesus. Allow the Holy Spirit to teach you everything that the Lord commands in the Bible. God wants us to let go of sin. If we truly are Christians, we will want to not sin and follow Jesus.

Homosexuality is a sin. We should love people unconditionally, but not condone sin in the church. If we are Christians, we will want to change inside and out. That involves a 180-degree turn, not looking back, and not running back to the same sins we are cleansed from. I am here to preach the truth, and the truth is that God hates sin, and it separates us from Him. How can we preach the word if we still hold onto what the Lord tells us to let go of?

I am not perfect, and I don't claim to be. Homosexuality is an abomination to God. He loves the people but hates the sin. Churches that allow same-sex marriages are not following what God wants. Pastors who support this will be judged. They should adhere to what the Bible says and not condone it. It is not okay. I am not the judge of the churches; that is God's job. But we need to stand firm on God's Word and preach the truth at all costs or suffer the consequences. I am saying this out of pure love for God's church.

There will be a cost for following Jesus. Let's not water down the Word. Rise up, church, and do not fall asleep, for the day of the Lord is near.

How have you suffered for following Jesus at all costs?

Prayer

'Dear heavenly Father, I pray that Your churches wake up and return to their first love to preach sound truth and doctrine, Father send forth Your spirit in the Last days to give Your church a message from You to love the people but not condone sin, I pray for father that You will be done here in America and the nations.'

FOLLOWING JESUS

Be ye followers of me, even as I also am of Christ.

Now I praise you, brethren, that ye remember me in all things, and keep the ordinances, as I delivered them to you. **1 Corinthians 11:1-2**

For even hereunto were ye called: because Christ also suffered for us, leaving us an example, that ye should follow his steps. **1 Peter 2:21**

Then spake Jesus again unto them, saying, I am the light of the world: he that followeth me shall not walk in darkness, but shall have the light of life. **John 8:12**

My sheep hear my voice, and I know them, and they follow me. **John 10:27**

And he saith unto them, Follow me, and I will make you fishers of men. **Matthew 4:19**

Now when Jesus heard these things, he said unto him, Yet lackest thou one thing: sell all that thou hast, and distribute unto the poor, and thou shalt have treasure in heaven: and come, follow me. **Luke 18:22**

This spake he, signifying by what death he should glorify God. And when he had spoken this, he saith unto him, Follow me. **John 21:19**

Surely goodness and mercy shall follow me all the days of my life: and I will dwell in the house of the LORD forever. **Psalm 23:6**

Then said Jesus unto his disciples, If any man will come after me, let him deny himself, and take up his cross, and follow me. **Matthew 16:24**

And as he passed by, he saw Levi the son of Alphaeus sitting at the receipt of custom, and said unto him, Follow me. And he arose and followed him. **Mark 2:14**

INTRODUCTION FREEDOM FROM SIN

Jesus died on the cross for our sins to be forgiven. He gave us freedom from sin by doing this. We were justified and sanctified by the blood of the Lamb. Freedom from our sins cost Jesus His life. Sin separates us from God. Can we continue to sin? The answer is no. We fall short, but the Lord gives us grace and mercy. We have to live a holy life. When sin comes our way, let's run from it as far as the East is from the West. The Holy Spirit will give us freedom.

How has the Lord given you freedom from sin? He gave me freedom from my past life. I will no longer be a slave to sin. He took my drugs and alcohol upon Himself to grant me a better life. He will also use us to teach people the importance of running away from sin. So, why do we tend to hold onto sin? He paid the price for us to be redeemed; He gave us freedom.

I am the first to admit I am a sinner saved by His transforming grace. I fall short, but His mercy and grace are enough to be forgiven. We all fall short; there is no one who is sin-free. Jesus was the only one who was blameless and without sin. We are all filthy rags standing in front of God, but He washes us, cleans us, and makes us white as snow. If we say we are without sin, we deceive ourselves, and the truth is not in us (1 John 1:8 KJV).

I heard a message almost four years ago from a speaker, and during the middle of his preaching, he said, "I live so high in the Spirit I cannot sin." Preaching is very dangerous. We put ourselves up on a pedestal. Jesus was the only one without sin. I will never forget what that minister said because he deceived himself and the minds of those who were listening to him. Be careful who you listen to. Always check for yourself if what people are preaching lines up with the Word of God. I knew what he said did not line up with God's Word, and I would not listen to that. I have come a long way. Do your research and read your Bible.

If people add to or twist the Word, what does it say in Revelation 22:18- 19? Anyone who adds things to the Word of God will have the plagues described in this scroll added to them, and if anyone takes words away, God will take away their share in the Tree of Life and in the holy city. Do not twist Scripture; the Bible is clear on this.

I have to be careful with this. I am an ordained minister, and not all should teach because we are held more accountable. God will give us freedom from sin, but let's not say that we are sin-free—we are not. There are sins we commit that we don't even know we commit.

How has Jesus given you freedom from your sins from your past life before you gave your life to him?

Prayer

'Dear heavenly Father, we come before your throne, we want to thank you for the freedom from our sins that you give us. It is not us cleansing ourselves, it's all you doing it. I ask you, Father, to continue to give us freedom from the sins we commit.'

FREEDOM FROM SIN

There is therefore now no condemnation to them which are in Christ Jesus, who walk not after the flesh, but after the Spirit.

For the law of the Spirit of life in Christ Jesus hath made me free from the law of sin and death. **Romans 8:1-2**

But now being made free from sin, and become servants to God, ye have your fruit unto holiness, and the end everlasting life. **Romans 6:22**

What then? shall we sin, because we are not under the law, but under grace? God forbid. **Romans 6:15**

Be it known unto you therefore, men and brethren, that through this man is preached unto you the forgiveness of sins:

And by him all that believe are justified from all things, from which ye could not be justified by the law of Moses. **Acts 13:38-39**

Help us, O God of our salvation, for the glory of thy name: and deliver us, and purge away our sins, for thy name's sake. **Psalm 79:9**

Being then made free from sin, ye became the servants of righteousness. **Romans 6:18**

For he that is dead is freed from sin. **Romans 6:7**

To him give all the prophets witness, that through his name whosoever believeth in him shall receive remission of sins. **Acts 10:43**

And now why tarriest thou? arise, and be baptized, and wash away thy sins, calling on the name of the Lord. **Acts 22:16**

Stand fast therefore in the liberty wherewith Christ hath made us free, and be not entangled again with the yoke of bondage. **Galatians 5:1**

Now the Lord is that Spirit: and where the Spirit of the Lord is, there is liberty. **2 Corinthians 3:17**

As far as the east is from the west, so far hath he removed our transgressions from us. **Psalm 103:12**

INTRODUCTION FRIENDSHIP

The friendships we build fill our lives with joy. A true friendship is rare—one that sticks closer than siblings. If you have that kind of friendship, never let it go. A friendship like that comes once in a lifetime. "Greater love hath no man than this, that a man lay down his life for his friends" (John 15:13 KJV). This was talking about Jesus, but if we do have a friend like that, never let them go.

Never let Jesus go—He is our true friend. Though man may reject us, though the church may reject us (and I have been rejected by a few churches), did it hurt? Of course, it did. I am here to tell you that Jesus was rejected, too. How can we expect not to be rejected? But Jesus will always be with us. He will never leave nor forsake us. Keep your friends close by; you never know when you are going to need them.

FRIENDSHIP

A man that hath friends must shew himself friendly: and there is a friend that sticketh closer than a brother. **Proverbs 18:24**

Greater love hath no man than this, that a man lay down his life for his friends. **John 15:13**

Iron sharpeneth iron; so, a man sharpeneth the countenance of his friend. **Proverbs 27:17**

Faithful are the wounds of a friend; but the kisses of an enemy are deceitful. **Proverbs 27:6**

A friend loveth at all times, and a brother is born for adversity. **Proverbs 17:17**

For if they fall, the one will lift up his fellow: but woe to him that is alone when he falleth; for he hath not another to help him up. **Ecclesiastes 4:10**

He that covereth a transgression seeketh love; but he that repeateth a matter separateth very friends. **Proverbs 19:9**

A froward man soweth strife: and a whisperer separateth chief friends. **Proverbs 16:28**

To him that is afflicted, pity should be shewed from his friend, but he forsaketh the fear of the Almighty. **Job 6:14**

Thine own friend, and thy father's friend, forsake not; neither go into thy brother's house in the day of thy calamity: for better is a neighbor that is near than a brother far off. **Proverbs 27:10**

Ye adulterers and adulteresses, know ye not that the friendship of the world is enmity with God? whosoever, therefore, will be a friend of the world is the enemy of God. **James 4:4**

INTRODUCTION GIVING AND TITHING

The Lord would like us to tithe 10 percent of our earnings. Any extra that we give beyond our tithe is an offering unto the Lord. There are blessings the Lord gives us when we tithe and give unto Him. The blessings that we receive from the Lord through tithing and giving might not necessarily be in the form of money. It could be better health, restored relationships, a better job, a favor, or even finding a good deal at a thrift store. Blessings from tithing can be many things. The Lord will prosper us, but not necessarily with money.

I don't preach a prosperity message of "give and you get rich." It doesn't work that way all the time. I have received blessings from the Lord, and it has not always been a lot of money. I don't care to get rich off God's Word. When we do tithe, we do get blessed. For example, a few years back, I had joined a ministry, and a week later, I got a raise at my job, even though I wasn't expecting one. That is how the Lord works when we tithe and make an offering unto Him. If we tithe to get rich, then we are doing it for all the wrong reasons. I tithe because I love the Lord and follow what the Bible says, not to get rich off God's Word. I tithe because I am being obedient to what the Word of God says, and blessings will follow.

I am a giver. In my past life, I was not a giver. I usually took it and was very disgraceful. But when the Lord came into me and I changed my life, I became a faithful giver. I would give a person the shirt off my back if they needed it. For the last four years, my family and I have held a garage sale during the city-wide garage sales. We receive donations from the community, and we give all the donations away. I talk to people about God and what He has done in my life, and I hand out gospel tracts. I once sat down with an older gentleman for about two hours, just talking to him about God and Jesus. He was not ready to receive, but the seed was planted. That is all that matters; God will do the work.

My dad has a testimony of giving a coworker a tract. Thirty years later, my dad ran into him, and the man told him that the tract he gave at work saved his life. He gave his life to Jesus. Praise God! There is power in gospel tracts. I am praying for God to use me in any way He can. I pray for opportunities to arise. Just recently, I gave to a ministry and provided pants for a homeless man. Then the Lord blessed me with professional paint for $11 a gallon, and I bought five of them. My mom and I were just talking about painting my house, and then the Lord provided 5 gallons of paint for $55. The thrift store also had a book sale—10 cents per book! I was so joyful for what the Lord did for me. Blessings can come in any way, and if money doesn't come, that's okay. I'm fine with small blessings. To me, they are big blessings from the Lord. Just don't give up and expect to get rich.

How has the Lord blessed you by tithing and offerings unto the Lord? Has it come back as money or in other ways?

Prayer

'Dear heavenly Father, thank you for the blessings that you have given us for being obedient to Your Word, to give back to you what you have given us, Father. God, it's a joy to give to other people when they need it. I pray, Father, that you continue to do a good work through us in Jesus Christ's holy name. I pray, Amen.'

GIVING AND TITHING

Every man according as he purposeth in his heart, so let him give; not grudgingly, or of necessity: for God loveth a cheerful giver. **2 Corinthians 9:7**

I have shewed you all things, how that so laboring ye ought to support the weak, and to remember the words of the Lord Jesus, how he said, It is more blessed to give than to receive. **Acts 20:35**

He that hath pity upon the poor lendeth unto the LORD, and that which he hath given will he pay him again. **Proverbs 19:17**

Honor the LORD with thy substance, and with the firstfruits of all thine increase.

So shall thy barns be filled with plenty, and thy presses shall burst out with new wine. **Proverbs 3:9-10**

The wicked borroweth, and payeth not again: but the righteous sheweth mercy, and giveth. **Psalm 37:21**

He coveteth greedily all the day long: but the righteous giveth and spareth not. **Proverbs 21:26**

There is that scattereth, and yet increaseth, and there is that withholdeth more than is meet, but it tendeth to poverty. **Proverbs**

11:24

Thus speak unto the Levites, and say unto them, When ye take of the children of Israel the tithes which I have given you from them for your inheritance, then ye shall offer up a heave offering of it for the LORD, even a tenth part of the tithe. **Numbers 18:26**

And all the tithe of the land, whether of the seed of the land or of the fruit of the tree, is the LORD's: it is holy unto the LORD. **Leviticus 27:30**

And this stone, which I have set for a pillar, shall be God's house: and of all that thou shalt give me, I will surely give the tenth unto thee. **Genesis 28:22**

And he looked up and saw the rich men casting their gifts into the treasury.

And he saw also a certain poor widow casting in thither two mites.

And he said, Of a truth I say unto you, that this poor widow hath cast in more than they all:

For all these have of their abundance cast in unto the offerings of God: but she of her penury hath cast in all the living that she had. **Luke 21:1- 4**

I fast twice a week, I give tithes of all that I possess. **Luke 18:21**

But woe unto you, Pharisees! for ye tithe mint and rue and all manner of herbs, and pass over judgment and the love of God: these ought ye to have done, and not to leave the other undone. **Luke 11:42**

Thou shalt surely give him, and thine heart shall not be grieved when thou givest unto him: because that for this thing the LORD thy God shall bless thee in all thy works, and in all that thou puttest thine hand unto. **Deuteronomy 15:10**

And Abel, he also brought of the firstlings of his flock and of the fat thereof. And the LORD had respect unto Abel and to his offering:

But unto Cain and to his offering he had not respect. And Cain was very wroth, and his countenance fell. **Genesis 4:4-5**

This they shall give, everyone that passeth among them that are numbered, half a shekel after the shekel of the sanctuary: (a shekel is twenty gerahs) a half shekel shall be the offering of the LORD. **Exodus 30:13**

Bring ye all the tithes into the storehouse, that there may be meat in mine house, and prove me now herewith, saith the LORD of hosts, if I will not open you the windows of heaven, and pour you out a blessing, that there shall not be room enough to receive it. **Malachi 3:10**

GOD'S DIRECTION AND PATH

God wants to lead you in the direction and path He wants you to be on. All we have to do is pray and seek His will and direction. He will put you on the path that leads to victory. Our path is not necessarily God's path; we have to understand that God is in charge, not us. When we rely on our own strength, it leads to failure or destruction. My friend, God wants to lead you on His path. Don't rely on your own strength (John 15:5).

When we rely on our own strength, it may work for a little while, but if our strength is not God's strength, it will lead us down a path to failure. God does not want you to fail; He wants you to succeed. I can recall a situation where I desperately needed God's direction. I got a call from a friend, and after our conversation, I had a question for God: "Do You really want me to go down this path?" I went to my parents' house early the next day. I was praying before breakfast, asking God, "Do You really want me to pick back up my studies in ministry?" I picked a promise out of a promise box. It was Isaiah 30:19-23, and it was confirmation that I was supposed to go back to my studies. I had heard the voice of the Lord through a promise God had given me: "Whether you turn to the right or the left, your ears will hear a voice behind you, saying, 'This is the way; walk in it.'"

When we seek God's direction and pray, God will answer us and put us on the path that leads in the right direction (Proverbs 3:5-6). Allow the Holy Spirit to guide you in every situation. The Spirit will guide you on your path in every situation that arises. God is so good; He will not let you stumble and fall (Psalm 37:24). Allow the Holy Spirit to guide you into all truth, and God will shine brightly in your life.

Which path does God have you on, and how can you rely on the Holy Spirit to guide you on the right path you're to be on?

Prayer

'Heavenly Father, we thank You for always guiding our steps and the paths You want us on. Please, Father, continue to guide our steps to the road to victory. We ask You, Father, to be the center of our life and to always rely on You when we need guidance on the path we need to be on. In Jesus Christ's name, we pray, Amen.'

INTRODUCTION GOSSIP

We should refrain from gossiping as much as we can. It can ruin a man's or woman's reputation. Plenty of times, I have been in conversations I should not have been in. The best way to avoid this is to simply not do it. If you enter a circle of people and you know gossip will happen, run from it and avoid it. Gossip is a sin.

In my past life, I used to gossip a lot. I was in the center of the ring, talking about people. If you talk about people, even if it is good and they are not there, it's still gossip. Flee from it and keep it to yourself. They might not want the news they told you to go around. Gossip may ruin a friendship. When you flee from talking about people, it builds your character and draws you closer to God. You do not want people to think of you as a busybody. When we gossip, it shows people that we are not trustworthy. Just don't gossip—find ways to flee from it.

Was there a time in your life when gossip ruined a friendship? How did you bounce back from that?

Prayer

'Heavenly Father, when the situation arises, please show us ways to avoid gossip, so we can find peace within you.'

GOSSIP

Let no corrupt communication proceed out of your mouth, but that which is good to the use of edifying, that it may minister grace unto the hearers. **Ephesians 4:29**

A froward man soweth strife: and a whisperer separateth chief friends. **Proverbs 16:28**

Thou shalt not raise a false report: put not thine hand with the wicked to be an unrighteous witness. **Exodus 23:1**

Whoso keepeth his mouth and his tongue keepeth his soul from troubles. **Proverbs 21:23**

If any man among you seem to be religious and bridleth not his tongue, but deceiveth his own heart, this man's religion is vain. **James 1:26**

The words of a talebearer are as wounds, and they go down into the innermost parts of the belly.

Burning lips and a wicked heart are like a potsherd covered with silver dross. Proverbs **26:22-23**

Speak not evil one of another, brethren. He that speaketh evil of his brother, and judgeth his brother, speaketh evil of the law, and judgeth the law: but if thou judge the law, thou art not a doer of the law, but a judge. **James 4:11**

A hypocrite with his mouth destroyeth his neighbor: but through knowledge shall the just be delivered. **Proverbs 11:9**

The words of a talebearer are as wounds, and they go down into the innermost parts of the belly. **Proverbs 18:8**

Death and life are in the power of the tongue: and they that love it shall eat the fruit thereof. **Proverbs 18:21**

Thou shalt not go up and down as a talebearer among thy people: neither shalt thou stand against the blood of thy neighbor; I am the LORD. **Leviticus 19:16**

He that hideth hatred with lying lips, and he that uttereth a slander, is a fool. **Proverbs 10:18**

But I say unto you, That, every idle word that men shall speak, they shall give account thereof in the day of judgment. **Matthew 12:36**

To speak evil of no man, to be no brawlers, but gentle, shewing all meekness unto all men. **Titus 3:2**

And withal they learn to be idle, wandering about from house to house; and not only idle but tattlers also and busybodies, speaking things which they ought not. **1 Timothy 5:13**

A false witness shall not be unpunished, and he that speaketh lies shall not escape. **Proverbs 19:5**

Keep thy tongue from evil, and thy lips from speaking guile.

Depart from evil, and do good; seek peace, and pursue it. **Psalm 34:13-14**

INTRODUCTION GUIDANCE

God will guide us; all we have to do is ask Him for the right way to go, how to speak to people, and how to handle situations that we get into. My friend, the Holy Spirit, will always guide and lead you. The straight and narrow path is there. Is there a certain time in your life when you needed guidance, and the Holy Spirit came through? We need a nudge from God every day in our lives. I ask Him every day for His perfect guidance to lead me on a straight path. I am praying for you, for God to show you which way to go.

Was there a time in your life when you needed guidance from the Holy Spirit on which way to go?

Prayer

'Heavenly Father, I pray that You guide us to where we need to go and show us which way when we don't know, as we ask You our Father. In Jesus Christ's name, we pray, Amen.'

GUIDANCE

And thine ears shall hear a word behind thee, saying, This is the way, walk ye in it, when ye turn to the right hand, and when ye turn to the left. **Isaiah 30:21**

And the LORD shall guide thee continually, and satisfy thy soul in drought, and make fat thy bones: and thou shalt be like a watered garden, and like a spring of water, whose waters fail not. **Isaiah 58:11**

I will instruct thee and teach thee in the way which thou shalt go: I will guide thee with mine eye. **Psalm 32:8**

If any of you lack wisdom, let him ask of God, that giveth to all men liberally, and upbraideth not; and it shall be given him.

But let him ask in faith, nothing wavering. For he that wavereth is like a wave of the sea driven with the wind and tossed. **James 1:5-6**

Thou shalt guide me with thy counsel, and afterward receive me to glory. **Psalm 73:24**

For thou art my rock and my fortress; therefore, for thy name's sake lead me, and guide me. **Psalm 31:3**

Thus, saith the LORD, thy Redeemer, the Holy One of Israel; I am the LORD thy God which teacheth thee to profit, which leadeth thee by the way that thou shouldest go. **Isaiah 48:17**

I will bless the LORD, who hath given me counsel: my reins also instruct me in the night seasons.

I have set the LORD always before me: because he is at my right hand, I shall not be moved. **Psalm 16:7-8**

And I will give you pastors according to mine heart, which shall feed you with knowledge and understanding. **Jeremiah 3:15**

To him the porter openeth; and the sheep hear his voice: and he calleth his own sheep by name, and leadeth them out.

And when he putteth forth his own sheep, he goeth before them, and the sheep follow him: for they know his voice. **John 10:3-4**

Order my steps in thy word: and let not any iniquity have dominion over me. **Psalm 119:133**

Teach me to do thy will; for thou art my God: thy spirit is good; lead me into the land of uprightness. **Psalm 143:10**

To give light to them that sit in darkness and in the shadow of death, to guide our feet into the way of peace. **Luke 1:79**

For this God is our God forever and ever: he will be our guide even unto death. **Psalm 48:14**

INTRODUCTION GRACE

What does it mean to have God's grace in your life? It means everything. Grace is freely given, even when we don't deserve it. When Jesus went to the cross to die for us, that, my friend, was God's grace for all of us. We are saved by grace (Ephesians 2:8-10 KJV). For by the grace of God, Jesus gave His life as a ransom so that we may truly live and have eternal life. We owe Jesus everything for laying His life down for us. How can we thank Him for the grace He has given us? We can't thank Him enough.

God's grace for my life was to redeem me from drugs and alcohol. I should be dead, but His grace was more sufficient than my sins. His grace redeemed us from the law; we are no longer under it. God's grace is eternal. We are no longer slaves to sin (Romans 6:1-7 KJV). We are saved by grace, not by our good works.

How can we give others grace who need things? If we don't help them, then God is not working in us. If we see a brother in need and do nothing about it, God's love is not displayed. I try to help as many as I can. Then, my friend, God gives us grace. Think of ways you can help people, and then God will help us when we need it.

There are many times when God gave me grace. In the winter of 2016, here in Iowa, I was driving to drop my son off to see his mother. It was March, the weather was good, and the skies were blue. On our way home, it started snowing, and the roads became icy and snow-packed. I was about an hour from home. My car started sliding; I was only going about 35 MPH. A snow plow was stopped at a stop sign, and my vehicle went out of control. I slid into the snow plow. I could have died, but thank God for looking out for me. My dad was with me. My hood blew off at the point of impact, the front end was smashed up, and the windshield was smashed. Angels were protecting my dad and me. God's grace kept us both alive. It could have been worse. A vehicle can be replaced; a life cannot.

Looking back on that day, I knew God kept me alive for this very purpose: to do the Lord's work and write this book for the body of Christ and the nations. I want to remain steadfast in God's Word and show the world how far the Lord has taken me, not me leading myself. I have tried leading myself, and it got me nowhere. God's grace has reminded me to stay humble and focused on the Holy Spirit. By God's grace, we all rejoice. There is plenty of work to do for the Lord right here in America, the land of the free and the home of the brave. Pray for America.

Just think, if we all stood up and prayed for America, God could give us grace. The local bodies need to start prayer groups for intercession for the nations. America is a nation in decline of the gospel. Read Genesis 18:16-33 KJV—Abraham intercedes for Sodom. There are millions of Christians in America. If we all intercede for America, God could give us grace and heal our land (2 Chronicles 7:14 KJV). If we would intercede for our country here in America, God could give us grace. Does America deserve punishment from God? Maybe. We are a nation that has gone far away from God's Word. Judgment starts with God's people first. We need to pray for America, for grace—He could give it to us.

I love this country, and I love God. If we took at least 15 minutes per day to pray for America and the nations, God's glory could show up. His grace and mercy may give us the grace we need. I cry for our nations to turn away from wickedness and turn to Jesus. Choose whom this day you want to serve (Joshua 24:15 KJV). We can only serve one master, and I choose to serve the Man who gave me eternal life—Jesus Christ, my Lord and Savior.

Our churches need to stand up for truth and stop condoning sin. Address it out of love. The churches that encourage same-sex marriages will not get grace when needed. I am not here to water down God's Word; I am here to bring His Word to life. The churches that allow same-sex marriage will be judged. The pastors who marry them will be judged. I'm here to share the Good News. That is an abomination to God in His church. Sin is sin. There is no sin greater than any other sin, except dying without Jesus. Churches that allow same-sex marriages will answer to God.

America has become modern-day Babylon, and Satan is behind the pulpit, controlling the church. We need to stand up for the truth or suffer the consequences. We have a choice to make: do we want to condone sin in the church, or do we want to let it go? God is not happy with how some churches have become. If we stand up for truth and do not condone sin, God may give our country, here in America, grace. I love God. I am His ambassador, called to stand up for truth at all costs. We all have a choice to make. Let's make the right choice to stand on God's Word. America was built on God's Word. What has happened to this country? Let's pray for America to change.

How has the Lord given you grace in your life? What was the outcome? Did you thank him?

Prayer

'Dear heavenly Father, please give us grace here in America as we stand up for truth, for Your Word, allow us to do mighty works for you'

181

GRACE

But Noah found grace in the eyes of the LORD. **Genesis 6:8**

For by grace are ye saved through faith; and that not of yourselves: it is the gift of God.

Not of works, lest any man should boast. **Ephesians 2:8-9**

But he giveth more grace. Wherefore he saith, God resisteth the proud, but giveth grace unto the humble. **James 4:6**

For sin shall not have dominion over you: for ye are not under the law, but under grace. Romans 6:14

And if by grace, then is it no more of works: otherwise grace is no more grace. But if it be of works, then it is no more grace: otherwise, work is no more work. **Romans 11:6**

But by the grace of God, I am what I am: and his grace which was bestowed upon me was not in vain; but I labored more abundantly than they all: yet not I, but the grace of God which was with me. 1 **Corinthians 15:10**

And of his fulness have all we received, and grace for grace. John 1:16

Being justified freely by his grace through the redemption that is in Christ Jesus. **Romans 3:24**

Thou, therefore, my son, be strong in the grace that is in Christ Jesus. **2 Timothy 2:1**

For the grace of God that bringeth salvation, hath appeared to all men,

Teaching us that, denying ungodliness and worldly lusts, we should live soberly, righteously, and Godly, in this present world. **Titus 2:11- 12**

And Joseph found grace in his sight, and he served him: and he made him overseer over his house, and all that he had he put into his hand. **Genesis 39:4**

And the LORD said unto Moses, I will do this thing also that thou hast spoken: for thou, hast found grace in my sight, and I know thee by name. **Exodus 33:17**

Who art thou, O great mountain? before Zerubbabel thou shalt become a plain: and he shall bring forth the headstone thereof with shoutings, crying, Grace, grace unto it. **Zechariah 4:7**

And I have oxen, and asses, flocks, and menservants, and womenservants: and I have sent to tell my lord, that I may find grace in thy sight. **Genesis 32:5**

And he said unto him, If now I have found grace in thy sight, then shew me a sign that thou talkest with me. **Judges 6:17**

And Ruth the Moabitess said unto Naomi, Let me now go to the field, and glean ears of corn after him in whose sight I shall find grace. And she said unto her, Go, my daughter. **Ruth 2:2**

And now for a little space grace hath been shewed from the LORD our God, to leave us a remnant to escape, and to give us a nail in his holy place, that our God may lighten our eyes, and give us a little reviving in our bondage. **Ezra 9:8**

Thou art fairer than the children of men: grace is poured into thy lips: therefore God hath blessed thee forever. **Psalms 45:2**

Surely, he scorneth the scorners: but he giveth grace unto the lowly. **Proverbs 3:34**

Thus, saith the LORD, The people which were left of the sword found grace in the wilderness; even Israel, when I went to cause him to rest. **Jeremiah 31:2**

And the child grew, and waxed strong in spirit, filled with wisdom: and the grace of God was upon him. **Luke 2:40**

And the Word was made flesh and dwelt among us, (and we beheld his glory, the glory as of the only begotten of the Father,) full of grace and truth. **John 1:14**

For the law was given by Moses, but grace and truth came by Jesus Christ. **John 1:17**

And with great power gave the apostles witness of the resurrection of the Lord Jesus: and great grace was upon them all. **Acts 4:33**

Let us therefore come boldly unto the throne of grace, that we may obtain mercy, and find grace to help in time of need. **Hebrews 4:16**

Who hath saved us, and called us with a holy calling, not according to our works, but according to his own purpose and grace, which was given us in Christ Jesus before the world began. **2 Timothy 1:9**

For if ye turn again unto the LORD, your brethren, and your children shall find compassion before them that lead them captive, so that they shall come again into this land: for the LORD your God is gracious and merciful, and will not turn away his face from you if ye return unto him. **2 Chronicles 30:9**

The grace of our Lord Jesus Christ is with your spirit. Amen. **Philemon 25**

But not as the offense, so also is the free gift. For if through the offense of one many be dead, much more the grace of God, and the gift by grace, which is by one man, Jesus Christ, hath abounded unto many. **Romans 5:15**

INTRODUCTION HOLINESS

We should strive to be holy like God. However, we all fall short. We are not perfect. Being holy takes a lot of sacrifice and prayer, committing to God, and allowing the Holy Spirit to work in us. Run from sin as fast as you can. Holiness takes a lot of God to shine in us; we have to be an example.

How can we be holy if we continue to sin? God's grace gives us forgiveness when we sin, but we can't continue to commit the same sin over and over. There are consequences. My friend, God will give you the desire to live a holy life that is pleasing to Him. Be that saint God has called us to be. Did you know the word "Christian" is mentioned in the Bible only three times, while the word "saint" is mentioned over 60 times? We are called to be saints.

Holiness is an aspect of Christianity for us to work on, including our attitude and character. We should work out our salvation with fear and trembling (Philippians 2:12 KJV). God wants us to be holy because He is holy. We will work on our behalf to strive to be that holy saint, God has called us to be. God loves you, my friend.

When we are Holy, how has that shown others what kind of life we live and how the Holy Spirit's fruits are evident in our lives?

Prayer

'Heaving Father, show us Your holiness so we can live a Holy life as well work in us and through us so others can see You in us.'

HOLINESS

Follow peace with all men, and holiness, without which no man shall see the Lord. **Hebrews 12:14**

But as he which hath called you is holy, so be ye holy in all manner of conversation.

Because it is written, Be ye holy; for I am holy. **1 Peter 1:15-16**

But now being made free from sin, and become servants to God, ye have your fruit unto holiness, and the end everlasting life. **Romans 6:22**

For they verily for a few days chastened us after their own pleasure; but he for our profit, that we might be partakers of his holiness. **Hebrews 12:10**

Having therefore these promises, dearly beloved, let us cleanse ourselves from all filthiness of the flesh and spirit, perfecting holiness in the fear of God. **2 Corinthians 7:1**

I speak after the manner of men because of the infirmity of your flesh: for as ye have yielded your member's servants to uncleanness and to iniquity unto iniquity; even so, now yield your member's servants to righteousness unto holiness. **Romans 6:19**

That he would grant unto us, that we being delivered out of the hand of our enemies might serve him without fear

In holiness and righteousness before him, all the days of our life. **Luke 1:74-75**

And that ye put on the new man, which after God is created in righteousness and true holiness. **Ephesians 4:24**

Notwithstanding she shall be saved in childbearing if they continue in faith and charity and holiness with sobriety. **1 Timothy 2:15**

Who is like unto thee, O LORD, among the Gods? who is like thee, glorious in holiness, fearful in praises, doing wonders? **Exodus 15:11**

Give unto the LORD the glory due unto his name: bring an offering, and come before him: worship the LORD in the beauty of holiness. **1 Chronicles 16:29**

Thy testimonies are very sure: holiness becometh thine house, O LORD, forever. **Psalm 93:5**

Speak unto all the congregation of the children of Israel, and say unto them, Ye shall be holy: for I the LORD your God am holy. **Leviticus 19:2**

But ye are a chosen generation, a royal priesthood, a holy nation, a peculiar people; that ye should shew forth the praises of him who hath called you out of darkness into his marvelous light. **1 Peter 2:9**

And one cried unto another and said, Holy, holy, holy, is the LORD of hosts: the whole earth is full of his glory. Isaiah 6:3

There is none holy as the LORD: for there is none beside thee: neither is there any rock like our God. **1 Samuel 2:2**

For I am the LORD your God: ye shall therefore sanctify yourselves, and ye shall be holy; for I am holy: neither shall ye defile yourselves with any manner of creeping thing that creepeth upon the earth. **Leviticus 11:44**

According as he hath chosen us in him before the foundation of the world, that we should be holy and without blame before him in love. **Ephesians 1:4**

For God hath not called us unto uncleanness, but unto holiness. **1 Thessalonians 4:7**

And he said, Draw not nigh hither: put off thy shoes from off thy feet, for the place whereon thou standest is holy ground. **Exodus 3:5**

Sanctify yourselves, therefore, and be ye holy: for I am the LORD your God. **Leviticus 20:7**

And ye shall be holy unto me: for I the LORD am holy, and have severed you from other people, that ye should be mine. **Leviticus 20:26**

INTRODUCTION HEARING GOD'S VOICE

DAILY READING HEBREWS 1:1-4

Hearing God's voice is absolutely amazing. His voice will lead us down a path toward victory. We can hear His voice in many ways, such as through the Word of God, His still small voice, through nature, and sometimes through people. God is a gentleman; He speaks to us in ways that can help us on our path with our walk with Jesus.

How can you hear His voice? We have to be still and calm (Psalm 46:10). That is when He speaks to us. When we sit down and spend time with Him in prayer, reading the Bible, going to church, and being in fellowship with one another (Hebrews 10:25), we are more likely to hear Him.

I have heard God's voice in many ways. On one occasion, I was going through a battle, and I heard His voice. The Lord spoke to me, "Joshua, I love what you are doing; keep doing it." He calls us by name. What a promise that is (Isaiah 45:3)!

I encourage you to be still and listen to God's voice. Don't get distracted by the ways of the world. Set your mind on things above (Colossians 3:2). Allow the Holy Spirit to work in you to overcome the busyness of the world so you can hear God's voice. It will be refreshing for you.

How can we hear God's voice? How can you make time for God to speak to you?

Prayer

'Heavenly Father, please keep my heart focused on You, to tune out the ways of the world and not to get distracted so we can fully hear Your voice, we ask You, loving Father, to be our minds on You and to spend time with You so we can hear Your loving voice, in Jesus Christ's name, we pray, Amen.'

Have you ever heard God's Voice? In many situations, I have heard His voice. His Voice can come to you in many ways, through the Bible, His actual Voice, or through nature and signs, and wonders. I have heard God's Voice through my phone. Yes, the Holy Spirit can use technology to speak to us. We must be calm and still to hear God's Voice. Not letting the business of the world distract us. To hear God's Voice, there will not be a ripple in the water when He speaks to us. Let go of the distractions and the noise of the world.

One instance, I was driving to visit my parents while they were camping. The Holy Spirit came upon me, God told me to stop my vehicle. I stopped. God told me to look at a tree and look at it closely. If something is wrong with someone that you love dearly, it will shake them up. A few hours later, I went back to that tree and laid my hands on the tree and prayed. God, who is this that You are speaking of? God never told me who it was. This was back in July of 2022 on a weekend. I continued with my business.

I got a call from my mother a few days later. I am in the ER they are going to admit me to the hospital. I went to the hospital after work, my mother told me some devastating news. It was the worst news I have ever heard in my life. She told me a combination of her meds had given her pancreatitis. I thought about God speaking to me through the tree a few days prior to that. Her high blood pressure medicine, which she was on, and a combination of other prescribed drugs, had given her an illness. My mother and I were on the same high blood pressure medicine. It was God's way of telling me to change the medication.

About a week later, I went back to that tree to pray for my mother. This time, I noticed a bulge coming out of the side of the tree. The tree resembled a human figure. The bulge was coming out around the stomach area. I don't understand why God showed me that, and neither does my mother. We are still praying for healing. It is in God's hands. Remember that Satan can speak to us just like God can. We must be able to discern if it is God or the enemy.

How have you heard God's Voice? How has it been for you? It is replenishing and refreshing when we hear His still, small Voice.

Prayer

'Dear Heavenly Father, please help those who cannot hear Your Voice, let them hear You. Please help all of us become better listeners to Your Voice. The Bible says, My sheep hear my voice. In Jesus' name, Amen.'

HEARING GOD'S VOICE

My sheep hear my voice, and I know them, and they follow me. **John 10:27**

But he said, Yeah rather, blessed are they that hear the word of God, and keep it. **Luke 11:28**

And this voice which came from heaven we heard when we were with him in the holy mount. **2 Peter 1:18**

And he said, I heard thy voice in the garden, and I was afraid, because I was naked; and I hid myself. **Genesis 3:10**

And the LORD said unto Moses, Lo, I come unto thee in a thick cloud, that the people may hear when I speak with thee, and believe thee forever. And Moses told the words of the people unto the LORD. **Exodus 19:9**

And when Moses was gone into the tabernacle of the congregation to speak with him, then he heard the voice of one speaking unto him from off the mercy seat that was upon the ark of the testimony, from between the two cherubims: and he spake unto him. **Numbers 7:89**

Yet heard I the voice of his words: and when I heard the voice of his words, then was I in a deep sleep on my face, and my face toward the ground. **Daniel 10:9**

While it is said, Today, if ye will hear his voice, harden not your hearts, as in the provocation. **Hebrews 3:15**

Wherefore as the Holy Ghost saith, Today, if ye will hear his voice. **Hebrews 3:7**

Also, I heard the voice of the Lord, saying, Whom shall I send, and who will go for us? Then said I, Here am I; send me. **Isaiah 6:8**

Out of heaven, he made thee hear his voice, that he might instruct thee: and upon earth, he shewed thee his great fire; and thou heardest his words out of the midst of the fire. **Deuteronomy 4:36**

God, who at sundry times and in divers manners spake in time past unto the fathers by the prophets,

Hath in these last days spoken unto us by his Son, whom he hath appointed heir of all things, by whom also he made the worlds;

Who being the brightness of his glory, and the express image of his person, and upholding all things by the word of his power, when he had by himself purged our sins, sat down on the right hand of the Majesty on high. **Hebrews 1:1-3**

Call unto me, and I will answer thee, and show thee great and mighty things, which thou knowest not. **Jeremiah 33:3**

And thine ears shall hear a word behind thee, saying, This is the way, walk ye in it, when ye turn to the right hand, and when ye turn to the left. **Isaiah 30:21**

Moreover, he said unto me, Son of man, all my words that I shall speak unto thee receive in thine heart and hear with thine ears.

And go, get thee to them of the captivity, unto the children of thy people, and speak unto them, and tell them, Thus, saith the Lord GOD; whether they will hear, or whether they will forbear. **Ezekiel 3:10-11**

Whether it be good, or whether it be evil, we will obey the voice of the LORD our God, to whom we send thee; that it may be well with us, when we obey the voice of the LORD our God. **Jeremiah 42:6**

And it shall come to pass, if thou shalt hearken diligently unto the voice of the LORD thy God, to observe and to do all his commandments which I command thee this day, that the LORD thy God will set thee on high above all nations of the earth. **Deuteronomy 28:1**

INTRODUCTION HOPE

Our hope rests securely in the Lord, trusting He will do all He has promised. We have hope that the Lord will rescue us in our time of need. We have to pray that He will use us to be servants in our community, our church, and our unsaved loved ones. The hope that God gives us will manifest to others and be a light to the lost. In God, we shall put our hope.

Has there been a time when you lost hope and the lord came through and did what he promised?

'Heavenly Father, we put our hope in You. Please continue to do work in us to give others hope who need you. Loving Father, we pray for hope for our people in Jesus Christ's name, we pray.'

HOPE

Behold, the eye of the LORD is upon them that fear him, upon them that hope in his mercy. **Psalm 33:18**

Hope deferred maketh the heart sick: but when the desire cometh, it is a tree of life. **Proverbs 13:12**

Now the God of hope fills you with all joy and peace in believing, that ye may abound in hope, through the power of the Holy Ghost. **Romans 15:13**

There is one body, and one Spirit, even as ye are called in one hope of your calling;

One Lord, one faith, one baptism,

One God and Father of all, who is above all, and through all, and in you all. **Ephesians 4:4-6**

Blessed be the God and Father of our Lord Jesus Christ, which according to his abundant mercy hath begotten us again unto a lively hope by the resurrection of Jesus Christ from the dead. **1 Peter 1:3**

Wherefore gird up the loins of your mind, be sober, and hope to the end for the grace that is to be brought unto you at the revelation of

Jesus Christ. **1 Peter 1:13**

Remembering without ceasing your work of faith, labor of love, and patience of hope in our Lord Jesus Christ, in the sight of God and our Father. **1 Thessalonians 1:3**

For whatsoever things were written aforetime were written for our learning, that we through patience and comfort of the scriptures might have hope. **Romans 15:4**

To whom God would make known what is the riches of the glory of this mystery among the Gentiles; which is Christ in you, the hope of glory. Colossians 1:27

The eyes of your understanding being enlightened; that ye may know what is the hope of his calling, and what the riches of the glory of his inheritance in the saints. **Ephesians 1:18**

Let thy mercy, O LORD, be upon us, according as we hope in thee. **Psalm 33:22**

But I will hope continually, and will yet praise thee more and more. **Psalm 71:14**

And hope maketh not ashamed; because the love of God is shed abroad in our hearts by the Holy Ghost which is given unto us. **Romans 5:5**

The LORD taketh pleasure in them that fear him, in those that hope in his mercy. **Psalm 147:11**

I wait for the LORD, my soul doth wait, and in his word do I hope. **Psalm 130:5**

The LORD is my portion, saith my soul; therefore, will I hope in him. **Lamentations 3:24**

INTRODUCTION HATRED

Hate is a strong word. If we hate our brother or sister, then we can't love God; it's what the Bible says. I used to dislike many things, including my coworkers. I have learned to let go of the hatred I once had. All it does is hurt us.

Let's work on this and let go of the past. Holding onto hatred only brings us down and keeps us bound. The enemy then has a stronghold on us. I rebuke the strongholds the enemy has on us. We need to look forward and not look back. Look what happened to Lot's wife when she looked back—she turned into a pillar of salt (Genesis 19:26 KJV).

The Holy Spirit working in us will help us get over our past. When we do hate, we are living in the flesh; that is a worldly trait. We all live in the flesh at times and struggle with things. Allow the Holy Spirit to help us when the flesh becomes a struggle. I pray that we can overcome this hate.

Have you hated people before? How has the Holy Spirit helped you through this?

Prayer

'Dear heavenly Father, I pray for those who are still struggling with hatred. I pray, Father, that your Holy Spirit will help them break this. In Jesus Christ's name, I pray, Amen.'

HATRED

He that saith he is in the light, and hateth his brother, is in darkness even until now.

He that loveth his brother abideth in the light, and there is none occasion of stumbling in him.

But he that hateth his brother is in darkness, and walketh in darkness, and knoweth not whither he goeth because that darkness hath blinded his eyes. **1 John 2:9-11**

If the world hates you, ye know that it hated me before it hated you. **John 15:18**

Thou shalt not hate thy brother in thine heart: thou shalt in any wise rebuke thy neighbor, and not suffer sin upon him. **Leviticus 19:17**

Hate the evil, and love the good, and establish judgment in the gate: it may be that the LORD God of hosts will be gracious unto the remnant of Joseph. **Amos 5:15**

Then Amnon hated her exceedingly; so that the hatred wherewith he hated her was greater than the love wherewith he had loved her. And Amnon said unto her, Arise, be gone. **2 Samuel 13:15**

For we ourselves also were sometimes foolish, disobedient,

deceived, serving diverse lusts and pleasures, living in malice and envy, hateful, and hating one another. **Titus 3:3**

We know that we have passed from death unto life because we love the brethren. He that loveth not his brother abideth in death.

Whosoever hateth his brother is a murderer: and ye know that no murderer hath eternal life abiding in him. **1 John 3:14-15**

Ye that love the LORD, hate evil: he preserveth the souls of his saints; he delivereth them out of the hand of the wicked. **Psalm 97:10**

The fear of the LORD is to hate evil: pride, and arrogancy, and the evil way, and the froward mouth, do I hate. **Proverbs 8:13**

And ye shall be hated of all men for my name's sake: but he that endureth to the end shall be saved. **Matthew 10:22**

For that, they hated knowledge and did not choose the fear of the LORD. **Proverbs 1:29**

For the LORD, the God of Israel, saith that he hateth putting away: for one covereth violence with his garment, saith the LORD of hosts: therefore, take heed to your spirit, that ye deal not treacherously. **Malachi 2:16**

Hear the word of the LORD, ye that tremble at his word; Your brethren that hated you, that cast you out for my name's sake, said, Let the LORD be glorified: but he shall appear to your joy, and they shall be ashamed. **Isaiah 66:5**

INTRODUCTION HELPING OTHERS

We should do our best to help people in need. It is rewarding when we lend a hand to the needy. God will reward us for our kind deeds to people. God's Word says we are to help those in need. Do not let your left hand know what your right hand is doing. That your giving will be done in secret. God will reward you, but do not announce it with trumpets like the Pharisees did.

Has there been a time in your life when you helped someone in need? Did God reward you back in full?

Prayer

'Dear Heavenly Father, I pray that you will use us to help those who are struggling with needs. In Jesus' name, Amen.'

HELPING OTHERS

For the poor shall never cease out of the land: therefore, I command thee, saying, Thou, shalt open thine hand wide unto thy brother, to thy poor, and to thy needy, in thy land. **Deuteronomy 15:11**

Pure religion and undefiled before God and the Father is this, To visit the fatherless and widows in their affliction, and to keep himself unspotted from the world. **James 1:27**

He that hath pity upon the poor lendeth unto the LORD, and that which he hath given will he pay him again. **Proverbs 19:17**

Withhold not good from them to whom it is due, when it is in the power of thine hand to do it.

Say not unto thy neighbor, Go, and come again, and tomorrow, I will give; when thou hast it by thee. **Proverbs 3:27-28**

Look not every man on his own things, but every man also on the things of others. **Philippians 2:4**

And if thou draw out thy soul to the hungry, and satisfy the afflicted soul; then shall thy light rise in obscurity, and thy darkness be as the noon day:

And the LORD shall guide thee continually, and satisfy thy soul in drought, and make fat thy bones: and thou shalt be like a watered garden, and like a spring of water, whose waters fail not. **Isaiah 58:10-11**

He that giveth unto the poor shall not lack: but he that hideth his eyes shall have many a curse. **Proverbs 28:27**

But whoso hath this world's good, and seeth his brother have need, and shutteth up his bowels of compassion from him, how dwelleth the love of God in him? **1 John 3:17**

He that hath a bountiful eye shall be blessed; for he giveth of his bread to the poor. **Proverbs 22:9**

Open thy mouth, judge righteously, and plead the cause of the poor and needy. **Proverbs 31:9**

But if any provide not for his own, and especially for those of his own house, he hath denied the faith and is worse than an infidel. **1 Timothy 5:8**

What doth it profit, my brethren, though a man say he hath faith, and have not works? can faith save him?

If a brother or sister is naked, and destitute of daily food,

And one of you say unto them, Depart in peace, be ye warmed and filled; notwithstanding ye give them, not those things which are needful to the body; what doth it profit?

Even so, faith, if it hath not worked, is dead, being alone. **James 2:14- 17**

Learn to do well; seek judgment, relieve the oppressed, judge the fatherless, plead for the widow. **Isaiah 1:17**

He that despiseth his neighbor sinneth: but he that hath mercy on the poor, happy is he. **Proverbs 14:21**

Give to him that asketh thee, and from him that would borrow of thee turn not thou away. **Matthew 5:42**

Whoso stoppeth his ears at the cry of the poor, he also shall cry himself, but shall not be heard. **Proverbs 21:13**

And the people asked him, saying, What shall we do then?

He answereth and saith unto them, He that hath two coats, let him impart to him that hath none; and he that hath meat, let him do likewise. **Luke 3:10-11**

If thine enemy be hungry, give him bread to eat; and if he be thirsty, give him water to drink:

For thou shalt heap coals of fire upon his head, and the LORD shall reward thee. **Proverbs 25:21-22**

For he shall deliver the needy when he crieth; the poor also, and him that hath no helper.

He shall spare the poor and needy and shall save the souls of the needy.

He shall redeem their soul from deceit and violence: and precious shall their blood be in his sight. **Psalm 72:12-14**

Therefore, if thine enemy hunger, feed him; if he thirst, give him drink: for in so doing thou shalt heap coals of fire on his head. **Romans 12:20**

INTRODUCTION HEALING

God can heal; I do not doubt that. Does healing come supernaturally? Yes, it can. God can also use doctors to heal. Luke was a physician, so God can use them, too. If you need healing and have prayed about it with no results, don't lose hope and faith. It's all in God's time.

My mother needs healing; she has a heart condition called AFib. We have all been praying for her for a long time, asking Jesus to heal her. We will not lose our faith. She also has pancreatitis, and her health is not very good. My dad has dementia, and we are praying for him, too.

If you could be so kind as to lift my parents up in prayer for Jesus to heal them, I would greatly appreciate it. Please pray for a miracle for them and ask your church and other believers you are connected with to pray for a divine miracle that only comes from God. The Holy Spirit can perform miracles.

Please start a prayer chain for them and have faith, my friend. God hears your prayers. Pray always; Jesus won't let you down.

Have you ever received a miracle healing from God that was beyond the doctor's understanding?

Prayer

'Dear Heavenly Father, I come boldly before Your throne of grace. I pray that those who need healing are healed. Use us for Your glory to pray for people, for miracle healings, and to anoint them with oil. I pray, Father, for my parents and their healing. Supernaturally heal them, Father. Please cast out all infirmities and diseases. Touch them, God, to heal them, and also heal others. Use me, Father, to pray and lay hands on the sick and anoint them with oil for miracle healing. I pray, Father, that Your will be done. Use us for Your glory to heal the sick in any way we can, healing them of their ailments. In Jesus Christ's name, I pray. Amen.'

HEALING

Heal me, O LORD, and I shall be healed; save me, and I shall be saved: for thou art my praise. **Jeremiah 17:4**

Have mercy upon me, O LORD; for I am weak: O LORD, heal me; for my bones are vexed. **Psalm 6:2**

Who his own self bare our sins in his own body on the tree, that we, being dead to sins, should live unto righteousness: by whose stripes ye were healed. **1 Peter 2:24**

Behold, I will bring it health and cure, and I will cure them and will reveal unto them the abundance of peace and truth. **Jeremiah 33:6**

O LORD my God, I cried unto thee, and thou hast healed me. **Psalm 30:2**

Is any sick among you? let him call for the elders of the church; and let them pray over him, anointing him with oil in the name of the Lord:

And the prayer of faith shall save the sick, and the Lord shall raise him up; and if he have committed sins, they shall be forgiven him.

Confess your faults one to another, and pray one for another, that ye may be healed. The effectual fervent prayer of a righteous man availeth much. **James 5:14-16**

And said, If thou wilt diligently hearken to the voice of the LORD thy God, and wilt do that which is right in his sight, and wilt give ear to his commandments, and keep all his statutes, I will put none of these diseases upon thee, which I have brought upon the Egyptians: for I am the LORD that healeth thee. **Exodus 15:26**

And ye shall serve the LORD your God, and he shall bless thy bread, and thy water, and I will take sickness away from the midst of thee. **Exodus 23:25**

 But he was wounded for our transgressions, he was bruised for our iniquities: the chastisement of our peace was upon him, and with his stripes, we are healed. **Isaiah 53:5**

I said, LORD, be merciful unto me: heal my soul; for I have sinned against thee. **Psalm 41:4**

He healeth the broken in heart, and bindeth up their wounds. **Psalms 147:3**

And Jesus went about all the cities and villages, teaching in their synagogues, preaching the gospel of the kingdom, and healing every sickness and every disease among the people. **Matthew 9:35**

And he said unto her, Daughter, thy faith hath made thee whole; go in peace, and be whole of thy plague. **Mark 5:34**

And the whole multitude sought to touch him: for there went virtue out of him, and healed them all. **Luke 6:19**

And he sent them to preach the kingdom of God, and to heal the sick. **Luke 9:2**

There came also a multitude out of the cities round about unto Jerusalem, bringing sick folks, and them which were vexed with unclean spirits: and they were healed, everyone. **Acts 5:16**

INTRODUCTION HONESTY

Are we honest in everything we do and say, or do we stretch the truth just a little to either gain attention or to present ourselves as something we are not? I used to stretch the truth a lot. If we are telling the truth but stretching it just a little to exaggerate what really happened, then we are lying. God wants us to be honest in everything we do and say. If we do not tell the truth, it leads to sin.

We need to be honest in all situations. In my past, I lied almost daily, sometimes to fit in with a group or to make people think I was something I wasn't. Little did they know, I was just a person who liked to stretch the truth. Lying is not the right way to gain attention. If we lie, we have to keep covering up that lie, and when we are exposed, we lose trust. I have lost trust before. When we lose trust, it's hard to gain it back.

Just be honest with people, even when it hurts. When people see our true colors and recognize that we are not honest, they won't want anything to do with us. Allow the Holy Spirit to help you if you struggle with being honest, even if it will cost you something. Being honest develops Christian morals and character. Let's work on being honest. We are not of this world; we belong to heaven.

Has there been a time in your life when you were not honest? How did you get past that?

Prayer

'Heavenly Father, work in us so we can be honest at all times, so people can see you in us.'

HONESTY

Lying lips are abomination to the LORD: but they that deal truly are his delight. **Proverbs 12:22**

Providing for honest things, not only in the sight of the Lord but also in the sight of men. **2 Corinthians 8:21**

He that speaketh truth sheweth forth righteousness: but false witness deceit. **Proverbs 12:17**

A faithful witness will not lie: but a false witness will utter lies. **Proverbs 14:5**

Every man shall kiss his lips that giveth a right answer. **Proverbs 24:26**

Render therefore to all their dues: a tribute to whom tribute is due; custom to whom custom; fear to whom fear; honor to whom honor. **Romans 13:7**

For there is nothing covered, that shall not be revealed; neither hid, that shall not be known. **Luke 12:2**

But Peter said, Ananias, why hath Satan filled thine heart to lie to the Holy Ghost, and to keep back part of the price of the land?

Whiles it remained, was it not thine own? and after it was sold, was it not in their own power? why hast thou conceived this thing in thine heart? thou hast not lied unto men but unto God. **Acts 5:34**

Lie not one to another, seeing that ye have put off the old man with his deeds. **Colossians 3:9**

If we say that we have fellowship with him, and walk in darkness, we lie and do not the truth. **1 John 1:6**

If we say that we have not sinned, we make him a liar, and his word is not in us. **1 Joh1:10**

If we say that we have no sin, we deceive ourselves, and the truth is not in us. **1 John 1:8**

INTRODUCTION HUMILITY

We will be humiliated if we are in Christ; that's just the nature of being a Christian. In what ways have you been humiliated for Christ's sake? If the world laughs and mocks us for being a Christian, that is being humiliated, and that's okay. It will happen. We can be humiliated in many ways, such as people mocking us for praying over a meal. I can see persecution coming to the United States for following Christ, and it may come sooner than we think.

On June 9th, 2023, I went street evangelizing with a friend from church. We shared our faith, prayed for people, and passed out gospel tracts. It was an amazing time. That night, I had a dream of a man coming up to me and telling me, "You need to stop talking about Jesus, or else." I awoke and prayed over the dream. If we are in Christ Jesus, we will be persecuted and humiliated (2 Timothy 3:12 KJV). There may be a storm coming to the United States that will shock this nation and shake it more than it is now. We may see things we have never seen before.

The following night, I had another dream of being in a house. A man came up to me and said, "I don't like you; in fact, I hate you." Then he took my arm and broke it. You can count on being persecuted for your faith in Jesus. Will persecution like it is overseas come to the United States for being a Christian? It may; I believe it will. It could happen. Be prepared. How far will you go? Are you going to deny Jesus, or will we rise up and stand firm in our faith in Jesus? I would take a bullet for Jesus because He gave His life for me on the cross.

The United States has been blessed, but I can see persecution coming here in many shapes and forms. If someone puts a gun to our heads and tells us to deny Jesus, what will we do? I can tell you right now, I would tell them to go ahead and kill me. My mother had a dream about a year ago, people dressed in all black coming into her house and killing our entire family. We are rebuking this dream and praying against it. There will be Christians martyred for their faith, and it could be coming now or in future times.

The dreams I've had about being persecuted for my faith—that's okay. I will not deny the name of Jesus. Look at what happened after COVID-19 emerged in the United States: the riots across this country. It may get worse in the future. Remain steadfast in God's Word. Be humiliated for Christ. I am going to endure until the end, or will some people fade out? Let's stand up for righteousness. We know this world will get worse; the Bible says so. I believe we are truly in the last days (2 Timothy 3 KJV).

Take a good look around us. What is going on in this world, especially in America? It's getting bad. What is right is declared wrong, and what is declared wrong is right. That is crazy. Are we truly in the last days before the rapture? I believe so. God sent me to this world to give our people a message: remain in the Word, remain in Christ. If we are not, then destruction will come upon people—a stern warning for America. Repent, turn away from wickedness, or suffer the consequences. This is for all nations, not just the United States. God sent me here to take as many people with me to heaven as I can and to preach His Word, not to water it down.

Talk about humility: some people just did not see the gifts the Holy Spirit gave me. I went on an adventure to find the body that I fit into. My entire life, I have been handed the short stick. Jesus gave me His Holy Spirit. What can man do to us? The past five years have been a learning experience. It's better when people cut us down just to walk away and say nothing. We have a job to do: show people love and Christ living in us. It's evident that some people will not like us, maybe even hate us. We need to love them anyway and be nice to them. It will heap hot coals on their heads (Proverbs 25:21-22; Romans 12:20 KJV).

How have you been humiliated for having faith in Jesus and being a Christian? How will we handle this? Will we lash out or love them anyway?

Prayer

'Dear heavenly, be with us when we are humiliated and persecuted for our faith in You, let Your Holy Spirit dwell within us so we can stand up for You.'

HUMILITY

Humble yourselves in the sight of the Lord, and he shall lift you up. **James 4:10**

Be of the same mind one toward another. Mind not high things, but condescend to men of low estate. Be not wise in your own conceits. **Romans 12:16**

Put on, therefore, as the elect of God, holy and beloved, bowels of mercies, kindness, humbleness of mind, meekness, longsuffering. **Colossians 3:12**

By humility and the fear of the LORD are riches, honor, and life. **Proverbs 22:4**

Before destruction the heart of man is haughty, and before honor is humility. **Proverbs 18:12**

And he sat down, and called the twelve, and saith unto them, If any man desire to be first, the same shall be last of all, and servant of all. **Mark 9:35**

The fear of the LORD is the instruction of wisdom; and before honor is humility. **Proverbs 15:33**

He must increase, but I must decrease. **John 3:30**

Likewise, ye younger, submit yourselves unto the elder. Yea, all of you be subject one to another, and be clothed with humility: for God resisteth the proud, and giveth grace to the humble. **1 Peter 5:5**

Better it is to be of a humble spirit with the lowly than to divide the spoiled with the proud. **Proverbs 16:19**

Whosoever therefore shall humble himself as this little child, the same is greatest in the kingdom of heaven. **Matthew 18:4**

And whosoever shall exalt himself shall be abased, and he that shall humble himself shall be exalted. **Matthew 23:12**

When pride cometh, then cometh shame: but with the lowly is wisdom. **Proverbs 11:2**

For whosoever exalteth himself shall be abased, and he that humbleth himself shall be exalted. **Luke 14:11**

For I say, through the grace given unto me, to every man that is among you, not to think of himself more highly than he ought to think, but to think soberly, according as God hath dealt to every man the measure of faith. **Romans 12:3**

Surely, he scorneth the scorners: but he giveth grace unto the lowly. **Proverbs 3:34**

INTRODUCTION HEAVEN

We all long for heaven. What a glorious day that will be when we reunite with our loved ones. The big picture is meeting the person who created us—that is, God. We all have so many questions to ask God. Heaven will be forever, reigning with Jesus for eternity, praising and worshiping with the Father, Son, and the Holy Spirit, and with all the other saints who went before us.

How the new heaven and earth will look keeps us wondering what that will be like. Will we be free to roam the earth and go back into the new Jerusalem? I know the vile, the sexually immoral, the idolaters, the people who practice magic arts, and the evil ones are cast into hell. The righteous will never die. For those who accept Jesus, heaven awaits us. I can't wait to meet our Creator. For now, we have a job to do: to bring as many people with us to heaven and escape hell.

How do you anticipate what heaven will look like, and how can we bring others with us?

Prayer

'Dear heavenly Father, we so eagerly desire to get into heaven, send people to us so they can go to heaven to use us to expand Your kingdom.'

228

HEAVEN

In my Father's house are many mansions: if it were not so, I would have told you. I am going to prepare a place for you. **John 14:2**

In the beginning, God created the heavens and the earth. **Genesis 1:1**

We are confident, I say, and willing rather to be absent from the body, and to be present with the Lord. **2 Corinthians 5:8**

And Jesus said unto him, Verily I say unto thee, Today, shalt thou be with me in paradise. **John 23:43**

But now they desire a better country, that is, a heavenly: wherefore God is not ashamed to be called their God: for he hath prepared for them a city. **Hebrews 11:16**

And no man hath ascended up to heaven, but he that came down from heaven, even the Son of man which is in heaven. **John 3:13**

Nevertheless, we, according to his promise, look for new heavens and a new earth, wherein dwelleth righteousness. **2 Peter 3:13**

And I saw a new heaven and a new earth: for the first heaven and the first earth were passed away, and there was no more sea.

And I, John, saw the holy city, new Jerusalem, coming down from

God out of heaven, prepared as a bride adorned for her husband.

And I heard a great voice out of heaven saying, Behold, the tabernacle of God is with men, and he will dwell with them, and they shall be his people, and God himself shall be with them, and be their God.

And God shall wipe away all tears from their eyes; and there shall be no more death, neither sorrow, nor crying, neither shall there be any more pain: for the former things are passed away.

And he that sat upon the throne said, Behold, I make all things new. And he said unto me, Write: for these words are true and faithful. **Revelation 21:1-5**

Lay not up for yourselves treasures upon earth, where moth and rust doth corrupt, and where thieves break through and steal.

But lay up for yourselves treasures in heaven, where neither moth nor rust doth corrupt, and where thieves do not break through nor steal.

For where your treasure is, there will your heart be also. **Matthew 6:19- 21**

And he shewed me a pure river of water of life, clear as crystal, proceeding out of the throne of God and of the Lamb.

230

In the midst of the street of it, and on either side of the river, was there the tree of life, which bare twelve manners of fruits, and yielded her fruit every month: and the leaves of the tree were for the healing of the nations.

And there shall be no more curse: but the throne of God and of the Lamb shall be in it, and his servants shall serve him:

And they shall see his face, and his name shall be in their foreheads.

And there shall be no night there, and they need no candle, neither light of the sun; for the Lord God giveth them light: and they shall reign forever and ever. **Revelation 22:1-5**

INTRODUCTION HUSBAND AND WIFE

Husbands, love your wives. Treat her with dignity and respect. Your wife is there to love you. Honor your wife. I know there are struggles in marriages, but the holy spirit is there to help you. Wives submit themselves to their husbands, love them, and honor them with everything they do. The husband is the man of the household, and we should try to work out our differences. The Lord will be your mediator. I pray that every husband and wife who is reading this will love their spouse unconditionally and be able to work out their problems. If you do wrong, forgive them and reconcile.

How can you give your marriage to God, to honor your marriage?

Prayer

'Dear Heavenly Father, I pray for husbands and wives who are reading this to have a wonderful marriage and to put God in the center of their marriage. I pray, Father, that they will be able to work out any kind of difference. In Jesus' name. Amen.'

HUSBAND AND WIFE

Likewise, ye wives, be in subjection to your own husbands; that, if any obey not the word, they also may without the word be won by the conversation of the wives;

While they behold your chaste conversation coupled with fear.

Whose adorning let it not be that outward adorning of plaiting the hair, and of wearing of gold, or of putting on of apparel;

But let it be the hidden man of the heart, in that which is not corruptible, even the ornament of a meek and quiet spirit, which is in the sight of God of great price.

For after this manner in the old time the holy women also, who trusted in God, adorned themselves, being in subjection unto their own husbands:

Even as Sara obeyed Abraham, calling him lord: whose daughters ye are, as long as ye do well, and are not afraid with any amazement.

Likewise, ye husbands, dwell with them according to knowledge, giving honor unto the wife, as unto the weaker vessel, and as being heirs together of the grace of life; that your prayers be not hindered.

1 Peter 3:1-7

Let the husband render unto the wife due benevolence: and likewise, also the wife unto the husband.

The wife hath not the power of her own body, but the husband: and likewise, also the husband hath not the power of his own body, but the wife.

Defraud ye not one the other, except it is with consent for a time, that ye may give yourselves to fasting and prayer; and come together again, that Satan tempts you not for your incontinency. **1 Corinthians 7:3-5**

Wives, submit yourselves unto your own husbands, as unto the Lord.

For the husband is the head of the wife, even as Christ is the head of the church: and he is the saviour of the body.

Therefore, as the church is subject unto Christ, so let the wives be to their own husbands in everything.

Husbands, love your wives, even as Christ also loved the church, and gave himself for it. **Ephesians 5:22-25**

Marriage is honorable in all, and the bed undefiled: but whoremongers and adulterers God will judge. **Hebrews 13:4**

Therefore, shall a man leave his father and his mother, and shall cleave unto his wife: and they shall be one flesh. **Genesis 2:24**

Nevertheless, to avoid fornication, let every man have his own wife, and let every woman have her own husband. **1 Corinthians 7:2**

And unto the married I command, yet not I, but the Lord, Let not the wife depart from her husband:

But and if she departs, let her remain unmarried or be reconciled to her husband: and let not the husband put away his wife. **1 Corinthians 7:10- 11**

Wives, submit yourselves unto your own husbands, as it is fit in the Lord. **Colossians 3:18**

That he might sanctify and cleanse it with the washing of water by the word,

That he might present it to himself a glorious church, not having spot, or wrinkle, or any such thing; but that it should be holy and without blemish.

So, ought men to love their wives as their own bodies? He that loveth his wife loveth himself.

For no man ever yet hated his own flesh; but nourisheth and cherisheth it, even as the Lord the church:

For we are members of his body, of his flesh, and of his bones.

For this cause shall a man leave his father and mother and shall be joined unto his wife, and they two shall be one flesh.

This is a great mystery: but I speak concerning Christ and the church.

Nevertheless, let every one of you in particular so love his wife even as himself, and the wife see that she reverences her husband.
Ephesians 5:26-33

INTRODUCTION JOY

Joy is a fruit of the Spirit (Galatians 5:22-23 KJV). It is better to be joyful than to frown and be negative. It takes more muscles to frown than it does to smile. How many times could we have been more joyful instead of having a chip on our shoulder? In my past life, I had a chip on my shoulder quite a bit. We should try our best to be always joyful, even when we are going through struggles.

I definitely could have had more joy when I decided to give my life back to the Lord. I became a very joyful person. If we are following God, we can have all of the fruits of the Spirit. Some fruits we need to work on, and the Holy Spirit will help us achieve the fruits of the Spirit if we allow Him to work in us.

Are you a joyful person? Has the Holy Spirit given you much joy?

Prayer

'Dear heavenly Father, it's a joy to serve You and be with You, give us more of Your Joy so others can see the Joy You have given us.'

JOY

But the fruit of the Spirit is love, joy, peace, longsuffering, gentleness, goodness, and faith. **Galatians 5:22**

Whom having not seen, ye love; in whom, though now ye see him not, yet believing, ye rejoice with joy unspeakable and full of glory. **1 Peter 1:8**

And ye now therefore have sorrow: but I will see you again, and your heart shall rejoice, and your joy no man taketh from you. **John 16:22**

The LORD thy God in the midst of thee is mighty; he will save, he will rejoice over thee with joy; he will rest in his love, he will joy over thee with singing. **Zephaniah 3:17**

These things have I spoken unto you, that my joy might remain in you, and that your joy might be full. **John 15:11**

Go thy way, eat thy bread with joy, and drink thy wine with a merry heart; for God now accepteth thy works. **Ecclesiastes 9:7**

I say unto you, that likewise, joy shall be in heaven over one sinner that repenteth, more than over ninety and nine just persons, which need no repentance. **Luke 15:7**

I have no greater joy than to hear that my children walk in truth. **3 John 1:4**

Hitherto have ye asked nothing in my name: ask, and ye shall receive, that your joy may be full. **John 16:24**

The father of the righteous shall greatly rejoice: and he that begetteth a wise child shall have joy of him. **Proverbs 23:24**

Therefore, with joy shall ye draw water out of the wells of salvation. **Isaiah 12:3**

And now come I to thee; and these things I speak in the world, that they might have my joy fulfilled in themselves. **John 17:13**

But let all those that put their trust in thee rejoice: let them ever shout for joy because thou defendest them: let them also that love thy name be joyful in thee. **Psalm 5:11**

Restore unto me the joy of thy salvation, and uphold me with thy free spirit. **Psalm 51:12**

For the kingdom of God is not meat and drink, but righteousness, and peace, and joy in the Holy Ghost. **Romans 14:17**

Thy words were found, and I did eat them, and thy word was unto me the joy and rejoicing of mine heart: for I am called by thy name, O LORD God of hosts. **Jeremiah 15:16**

A man hath joy by the answer of his mouth: and a word spoken in due season, how good is it! **Proverbs 15:23**

Rejoice ye in that day, and leap for joy: for, behold, your reward is great in heaven: for in the like manner did their fathers unto the prophets. **Luke 6:23**

And there was great joy in that city. **Acts 8:8**

O come, let us sing unto the LORD: let us make a joyful noise to the rock of our salvation.

Let us come before his presence with thanksgiving, and make a joyful noise unto him with psalms. **Psalm 95:1-2**

And the angel said unto them, Fear not: for, behold, I bring you good tidings of great joy, which shall be to all people. **Luke 2:10**

And now shall mine head be lifted up above mine enemies round about me: therefore, will I offer in his tabernacle sacrifices of joy; I will sing, yea, I will sing praises unto the LORD. **Psalm 27:6**

And the ransomed of the LORD shall return, and come to Zion with songs and everlasting joy upon their heads: they shall obtain joy and gladness, and sorrow and sighing shall flee away. **Isaiah 35:10**

And the seventy returned again with joy, saying, Lord, even the devils are subject unto us through thy name. **Luke 10:17**

Be glad in the LORD, and rejoice, ye righteous: and shout for joy, all ye that are upright in heart. **Psalm 32:11**

INTRODUCTION JUSTIFICATION

Romans 3:21-31

Justification in Christian theology refers to the act of God declaring a sinner righteous. It occurs the moment we say yes to Christ and ask for forgiveness of our sins and repent and turn away and invite Jesus int our hearts. Justification is not based on our good works or the deeds we do for others; the Bible teaches us that we are justified by faith alone, and our faith leads to justification. Faith itself is a gift from God given by the Holy Spirit.

Justification happens at conversion when we turn to Jesus, repent of our sins, and invite Christ into our hearts to be our Lord and Savior. I experienced my justification on July 20th, 2019, at a Christian retreat. I went there under the influence of drugs, only to please my parents, and I was living a sinful life, unaware of the transformation that awaited me that night. I had a radical encounter with the Holy Spirit; I was alone in a pew, questioning why I was there. I did not want to change. I wanted to go home and do drugs. I don't know how long I was in the pew, but when I opened my eyes, I was kneeling at the altar, staring at the cross.

In that moment, I felt the hand of God touch me, and he spoke to me: "if you truly love me, go home and change your life." That, my friend, was enough to convince me that God was real and I needed to make a change. I repented of my sins and invited Jesus to come into my heart; I felt a warm blanket coming over me I was justified by the faith I put in him. After struggling with a twenty-two year-drug habit, Jesus delivered me, and I have been clean and sober for six years-praise God! Only Jesus can do that, he is my rehab. My life was turned upside down on July 20th, 2019, and I will never look back.

In these six years, I have learned a lot. I became an ordained minister, went on a mission trip to Liberia, Africa, and even wrote a book. God has used me in mighty ways, but he has also told me to remain humble. Have you been truly justified? Have you repented of your sins and invited Jesus into your heart? If you haven't, I pray that you do. Without this step, you have not been justified. We are continually justified by the blood of Jesus. I encourage you to make Jesus your Lord and Savior; if you have not, then you cannot be justified. Justification is the spiritual power that enables us to accept Jesus as our Lord and Savior, and Jesus is returning soon. Justification is made available to us through Christ's finished work on the cross. By faith we receive this gift.

I will continue to pray for you and for the nations to turn back to God and be justified by faith in Jesus. Remember, our good works will not get us into heaven; only faith in Jesus can do that. Will you allow the Holy Spirit to lead you into justification? If you haven't, my friend, know that God loves you and desires for you to have a relationship with Jesus Christ His Son.

Can you remember that moment when you accepted Jesus as your Lord and Savior and were Justified?

Heavenly Father, thank you for the gift of eternal life. I praise you for the justification I have through your blood that was shed on Calvary. I ask you Father, to reveal yourself to unbelievers so they may also be justified. Use us, God, to save those who are lost, so they can be justified in the name of Jesus Christ, I pray amen.

JUSTIFICATION

That being justified by his grace, we should be made heirs according to the hope of eternal life. **Titus 3:7**

And not only so, but we also joy in God through our Lord Jesus Christ, by whom we have now received the atonement. **Romans 5:11**

Knowing that a man is not justified by the works of the law, but by the faith of Jesus Christ, even we have believed in Jesus Christ, that we might be justified by the faith of Christ, and not by the works of the law: for by the works of the law shall no flesh be justified.

But if, while we seek to be justified by Christ, we ourselves also are found sinners, is, therefore, Christ the minister of sin? God forbid. **Galatians 2:16-17**

Therefore, we conclude that a man is justified by faith without the deeds of the law. **Romans 3:28**

Moreover, whom he did predestinate, them he also called: and whom he called, them he also justified: and whom he justified, them he also glorified. **Romans 8:30**

Who was delivered for our offences, and was raised again for our justification. **Romans 4:25**

245

Much more than, being now justified by his blood, we shall be saved from wrath through him. **Romans 5:9**

Wherefore the law was our schoolmaster to bring us unto Christ, that we might be justified by faith. **Galatians 3:24**

For if Abraham were justified by works, he hath whereof to glory; but not before God. **Romans 4:2**

Therefore, by the deeds of the law, there shall no flesh be justified in his sight: for by the law is the knowledge of sin. **Romans 3:20**

And by him all that believe are justified from all things, from which ye could not be justified by the law of Moses. **Acts 13:39**

And not as it was by one that sinned, so is the gift: for the judgment was by one to condemnation, but the free gift is of many offenses unto justification. **Romans 5:16**

JESUS' BLOOD PROTECTS US

Jesus' blood protects you from harm that may come your way. Trust the Lord that He will sustain you in times of trouble or potential harm that may come your way (2 Thessalonians 3:3), which speaks of how the Lord will establish you and guard you against the evil one. Satan wants to destroy you, but God will not allow it. He has His angels surrounding us. My friend, God wants you to always cover yourself with the blood of Jesus, whether you're driving, at work, boating, swimming, etc. Say a prayer and ask the Lord to cover you with the blood of the Lamb. The Holy Spirit will keep you free of any danger that may come your way.

One situation my son and I experienced was when we laid our hands on our vehicle and prayed, "Lord, protect us while we drive to our destination." I was almost at our destination when a vehicle pulled out in front of me, and we hit a truck at 55 miles per hour. If we had not prayed before we left, the outcome could have been worse. My son broke his collarbone, but nothing happened to me. It was a miracle; no one died, including the other driver (Psalm 138:7). The Lord preserved all of us. Satan wanted all of us dead; he hates us, but God is bigger than the enemy's schemes. The Holy Spirit will carry you through every potential disaster that comes your way. No weapon formed against you shall prosper (Isaiah 54:17). The Holy Spirit, which surrounds you, will keep you safe from the enemy

247

when he wants to destroy you. Allow the Holy Spirit to encircle you at all times, and always pray before you do anything.

In what situations can you pray for the Holy Spirit to protect you? How will you ask the Lord for help?

Prayer

'Heavenly Father, we thank You for sending Your son into the world for his blood to protect us from Satan and his demons. We pray Father for Your protection, for our livesY may your blood cover us and keep us safe from the enemy in Jesus Christ's name, we pray. Amen.'

INTRODUCTION LOVE

Love is a four-letter word that is supposed to build up people and the body of Christ. We are to love one another unconditionally, no matter what people do to us; we are to love them anyway. Let love be your greatest aim. One of the most powerful messages in the Bible is the new commandment Jesus gave to us: love the Lord with all of your heart, soul, and mind (Matthew 22:37 KJV), and love your neighbor as yourself. Then why can't we love people as Christ loved us? I fail at this a lot of times. We need to love them instead of pointing fingers. When we do this, remember that three fingers are pointing back at us.

Jesus did not come into the world to condemn the world; He came here to save the world (John 3:17 KJV). When I went on the retreat, I had a mountaintop experience. I was on top of the mountain for over three years, looking down at the world. I know I have mentioned this in another topic, but it still needs to be spoken about again. The entire process was not love; I condemned people, judged them, and pointed out all of their faults. I have many of my own faults. That is not love; it's being judgmental and acting like I was better than them. Love is supposed to bring people closer to God, and love is the greatest gift we can have. We misunderstand love.

I have learned more sitting in the valley. When I finally decided to come down and learn from Jesus, I grew closer to God through this process. Allow the Holy Spirit to show you what true love is.

How can we love people even when they despise us and ridicule us for our faith in Jesus? Is it easy to love them anyway?

Prayer

'Dear Heavenly Father, show us pure love so we can share that love with others. We pray that we are able to love them and show people compassion.'

LOVE

We love him because he first loved us.

If a man says, I love God and hateth his brother, he is a liar: for he that loveth not his brother whom he hath seen, how can he love God whom he hath not seen? **1 John 4:19-20**

Beloved, let us love one another: for love is of God; and every one that loveth is born of God, and knoweth God.

He that loveth not knoweth not God; for God is love. **1 John 4:7-8**

And we have known and believed the love that God hath to us. God is love, and he that dwelleth in love dwelleth in God, and God in him. **1 John 4:16**

With all lowliness and meekness, with longsuffering, forbearing one another in love. **Ephesians 4:2**

This is my commandment, That ye love one another, as I have loved you. **John 15:12**

And the Lord directs your hearts into the love of God, and into the patient waiting for Christ. **2 Thessalonians 3:5**

No man hath seen God at any time. If we love one another, God dwelleth in us, and his love is perfected in us. **1 John 4:12**

Since thou wast precious in my sight, thou hast been honorable, and I have loved thee: therefore, will I give men for thee, and people for thy life. **Isaiah 43:4**

Hatred stirreth up strifes: but love covereth all sins. **Proverbs 10:12**

And thou shalt love the Lord thy God with all thy heart, and with all thy soul, and with all thy mind, and with all thy strength: this is the first commandment.

And the second is like namely this, Thou, shalt love thy neighbour as thyself. There is no other commandment greater than these. **Mark 12:30-31**

But speaking the truth in love may grow up into him in all things, which is the head, even Christ. **Ephesians 4:15**

Who shall separate us from the love of Christ? shall tribulation, or distress, or persecution, or famine, or nakedness, or peril, or sword? **Romans 8:35**

But I say unto you, Love your enemies, bless them that curse you, do good to them that hate you, and pray for them which despitefully use you, and persecute you. **Matthew 5:44**

And above all things have fervent charity among yourselves: for charity shall cover the multitude of sins. **1 Peter 4:8**

And now abideth faith, hope, charity, these three; but the greatest of these is charity. **1 Corinthians 13:13**

INTRODUCTION MERCY

God gives us more mercy than we think. I can remember in the summer of 2009, I had a boil on my stomach. It progressively got bigger and bigger, and then my left knee started to swell up. My knee eventually became the size of a softball. I decided to go to the doctor, and I don't like going to the doctor. It turned out I had MRSA and a staph infection. I was admitted to the hospital. A joint specialist came into my room to look at my knee, and he told me, "If the infection went too deep, we may have to amputate your leg from the knee down." The biggest fear set in my life. I then prayed that God would give me mercy. I cried out to Him, even though I was not following God at the time.

After the test results came back, the infection did not go too deep. I was very thankful; it was a huge relief. My doctor told me that if I had waited a few more days to come in, it could have been worse. I was in the hospital for almost a week. While I was in the hospital, I remembered that in the summer of 1999, during a party, I was drinking with friends and carrying on. We thought it would be cool to go and buy an Ouija board. We took it out of the box and played around with it. I asked the Ouija board, "When am I going to die?" The oracle then moved to the number "2009," which was, ironically, the year I had the staph infection. It was no coincidence. I know Satan was trying to kill me. Playing around with the occult is not cool; we open a portal to hell that evil spirits come out of. Evil was trying to kill me—I know it was. That's why the oracle said "2009." I nearly died in the hospital that year. The entire year was not good, but God's plan is far bigger than Satan's plan. Never play around with those things and the occult because it is pure evil. God had given me mercy in 2009; He spared my life.

How has the Lord granted you mercy from things, and how has that given you a reason to share it?

Prayer

'Heavenly Father, grant us mercy in due time, keep the enemy far from our camp, and allow no evil to come upon us in Jesus' name.'

MERCY

Be ye therefore merciful, as your Father also is merciful. **Luke 6:36**
Blessed are the merciful: for they shall obtain mercy. **Matthew 5:7**

Blessed be the God and Father of our Lord Jesus Christ, which according to his abundant mercy hath begotten us again unto a lively hope by the resurrection of Jesus Christ from the dead. **1 Peter 1:3**

He hath shewed thee, O man, what is good; and what doth the LORD require of thee, but to do justly, and to love mercy, and to walk humbly with thy God? **Micah 6:8**

But go ye and learn what that meaneth, I will have mercy, and not sacrifice: for I am not come to call the righteous, but sinners to repentance. **Matthew 9:13**

But God, who is rich in mercy, for his great love wherewith he loved us,

Even when we were dead in sins, hath quickened us together with Christ, (by grace ye are saved) **Ephesians 2:4-5**

Have mercy upon me, O God, according to thy lovingkindness: according unto the multitude of thy tender mercies blot out my transgressions.

Wash me thoroughly from mine iniquity, and cleanse me from my sin. **Psalm 51:1-2**

Who is a God like unto thee, that pardoneth iniquity, and passeth by the transgression of the remnant of his heritage? he retaineth not his anger forever, because he delighteth in mercy. **Micah 7:18**

And therefore will the LORD wait, that he may be gracious unto you, and therefore will he be exalted, that he may have mercy upon you: for the LORD is a God of judgment: blessed are all they that wait for him. **Isaiah 30:18**

Remember, O LORD, thy tender mercies and thy loving kindnesses; for they have been ever of old.

Remember not the sins of my youth, nor my transgressions: according to thy mercy remember thou me for thy goodness' sake, O LORD. **Psalm 25:6-7**

Withhold not thou thy tender mercies from me, O LORD: let thy lovingkindness and thy truth continually preserve me. **Psalm 40:11**

Nevertheless, for thy great mercies' sake, thou didst not utterly consume them, nor forsake them; for thou art a gracious and merciful God. **Nehemiah 9:31**

He that covereth his sins shall not prosper: but whoso confesseth and forsaketh them shall have mercy. **Proverbs 28:13**

Let the wicked forsake his way, and the unrighteous man his thoughts: and let him return unto the LORD, and he will have mercy upon him; and to our God, for he will abundantly pardon. **Isaiah 55:7**

And David said unto Gad, I am in a great strait: let us fall now into the hand of the LORD; for his mercies are great: and let me not fall into the hand of man. **2 Samuel 24:14**

Know therefore that the LORD thy God, he is God, the faithful God, which keepeth covenant and mercy with them that love him and keep his commandments to a thousand generations. **Deuteronomy 7:9**

For he saith to Moses, I will have mercy on whom I will have mercy, and I will have compassion on whom I will have compassion. **Romans 9:15**

INTRODUCTION OBEDIENCE

Obedience to the Lord pays off. There are blessings in obeying the Lord. With obedience comes steadfastness. God wants us to always walk in upright paths, being obedient to the teachings of the gospel. We are called to be not only hearers of the Word but also doers of the Word. "Do what it says" (James 1:22 KJV). My friend, it is very important to be a doer of the Word, not only to hear it. When we walk in disobedience, God can punish us, and we do not want that. Try your very best to walk in obedience to God; He will surely bless you.

When I was in my early 20s, I was as disobedient as they came—doing drugs, smoking, having premarital sex, and not even living remotely close to a Godly life. I went on this path from the age of 19 until I was 40 years old. God changed everything in the blink of an eye in July 2019. I went on a Christian retreat for four days. A few days prior to the retreat, I was getting high. I had mentioned to the person I was doing drugs with that I was going on a Christian retreat. He told me, "Why do you want to go to something stupid like that?" I almost listened to him, but I went on the retreat anyway. I had to get high before I went.

When I arrived at the church, the pastors and staff knew I was under the influence of drugs. I heard voices saying, "You're going to listen

259

to 15 stupid speakers and go home and do the same old song and dance." The people there were all laughing and very joyful, and I thought, "What is wrong with these people?" I only wanted to please my parents by going to the retreat—nothing more than that. Little did I know what God had in store that weekend. I did not want to be there. I almost called my mother to come and get me because I wanted out. All I wanted to do was go home and do drugs.

It was Saturday, July 20th, 2019, at 10 pm. All of the retreat attendees were in the chapel, separated. I was sitting alone, depressed, broken, wondering why I was even there. I didn't want to change; I wanted to go home and do drugs. My eyes were closed as I sat alone in the pew. I can't remember how long I was sitting there. A few moments later, I opened my eyes and found myself kneeling at the altar, looking at the cross. The hand of God came down from heaven and touched me. I heard God's voice: "My son, if you truly love and want to be my humble servant, go home and change your life." That, my friend, was enough to convince me that God is real.

I then had to make a decision: to repent and turn away from my wickedness or go home and serve Satan. Three things happened that very hour and that second: I heard God's voice, I listened to Him, and I obeyed Him. We can't serve two masters; it's either God or Satan. We have a choice to make, and God made it very real to me to choose either life or destruction. That night, I had a radical encounter with the Holy Spirit. I made the decision to repent, ask for forgiveness of my sins, and invite Jesus to come into my heart and back into my life. I was a prodigal son, raised in church, but had fallen away. God forgave me, and I rededicated my life to the Lord. I had a 22-year drug habit, but God healed me that night, and He put His Spirit into me. Jesus has been my rehab.

When I gave my life back to the Lord, I could feel a warm blanket coming over and into me. That was the Holy Spirit; it was Jesus. If He can do this for me, He can do it for anyone who wants to change their life. We have to want to change. People can point it out, but we have to want to change. I know that a few days prior to the retreat, I was listening to the voice of Satan. If I had listened to him and not gone to the retreat, my transformation would have never happened. Looking back at the guys who were joyful and smiling, they had something I desperately needed and wanted—it was Jesus. I reached out and put Him into my heart. God saved me from drugs and a life of despair. I owe Jesus everything.

During the closing ceremonies at the retreat, the people who went through the first time were asked, "What does this retreat mean to you, and what will you do after you leave?" When it was my turn to go to the pulpit, I was very nervous. I can't remember what I said, but the Holy Spirit came upon me. What I do remember is that I said,

"It meant everything that God changed me, and the Holy Spirit came into my heart. Now I have a job to do, which is to proclaim the gospel at all costs and share my testimony" (Revelation 12:11 KJV). Leading others to the Lord was glorious in the sight of the Lord.

I didn't even realize I had a calling in my life until I went on this retreat. After my time at the pulpit, my table leader nudged me and said, "I can sense a preacher in you." His words inspired me to be the very best I can be. That was the encouragement I needed. I love him with all of my heart. We have talked on the phone for countless hours beyond the retreat. It is nice to have a friend like this to give wisdom and advice. He has helped me a lot. I call him almost every day. It is amazing having a friend like him; we were destined by God to meet.

After the retreat was over, I was leaving the church, and I heard a voice say, "Rebuild walls." God also told me Joshua 24:15. Upon leaving the church, I did not understand this until about five years later. When I went home, my family was eager to see me. I broke down, wept, and told them the good news of what had happened— that the Holy Spirit changed me. My dad and I did not see eye to eye for a long time. I told him, "I forgive you for the past; let's move forward and be father and son."

I looked up the scripture Joshua 24:15. It was the Holy Spirit telling me that I had been serving false gods for a long time. When God told me to change my life, I didn't realize He was going to change me inside and out. I called my dad and took all of my drugs over to his house. We built a fire, and I threw all of the drugs into the fire pit and burned them. I am very grateful for what the Lord did for me at the retreat.

The Holy Spirit made me who I am today. It was the Lord that did it, not me—I could not do this without Him.

God told me to go to my house and throw away everything that did not resemble the Lord. I threw away all of my football memorabilia, all of my secular music, and all of the posters on the wall that were secular. I threw away thousands of dollars' worth of stuff that did not mean a thing to me because I was serving the Lord and not Satan anymore. We can serve false gods without even realizing it. Anything we put before the Lord then becomes a false god and an idol. I had plenty of idols. I worshiped the NFL. After my transformation, it meant nothing. I followed football my entire life, writing stats down and not missing a game on TV. I could talk about football for an 8-hour workday. After my transformation to the Lord, I can talk about what God did for me all day long.

The day after the retreat, my son and I placed our hands on my Bible and put my cigarettes on it. We prayed, "God, please take this nasty habit away from me," and I threw them away. That day, I quit smoking and never went back. The Holy Spirit took my 22-year habit of smoking away in seconds. I thank Jesus for doing this for me. I have been smoke-free for five years. Years ago, my mother was upset when I started smoking, and she told me how she quit: "I placed my hand on my Bible and threw them away." At the time, I thought, "No way, I can never do that. You're crazy." Don't doubt what God can do. I did exactly what my mother told me she do, and I quit smoking. I relied on the Holy Spirit's strength and not my own power. I had tried quitting many times, but only God can do this.

Since the retreat, I have become an ordained minister. God has called me into ministry. I write for our town's local newspaper about six times per year. I am in rotation with the pastors in our community. God has used our family to save and lead people to the Lord. I have had many trials and afflictions. It was God doing this to teach me His way and not my own way. I will admit I can be stubborn and want it my way. But it's God's way or no way—our way leads to destruction.

In December of 2022, I received an associate's degree in Biblical Studies. It was hard work that paid off. I started this journey in 2019. I was super joyful when I completed my degree. God was well pleased with me for sticking this out. It was challenging, but when I started something, I always completed what I had started. My table leader's words came true: "I sense a preacher in you." It was a prophecy from him through the Lord that was fulfilled.

I called him on January 9th, 2021, afterwords from a pastor I am connected with who spoke to me on January 6th, 2021. The Capitol riots happened in America on that sorrowful day. The words that were spoken to me came from Ezekiel 33:21-33. Two nights later, on January 8th, I had a dream, and I decided to call him about it. I was standing around a building that resembled our nation's structure, our nation's Capitol. The building was in total ruins and destruction. I was preaching a message of hope to God's people that we have to make a decision to serve God or Satan. There was complete silence for a few seconds. I am writing a book for America to decide to serve God and to go back to our first love. Is there hope for America? I hope so.

Ever since I called him that day, I have been reading his book to him in the Spirit. Everything I have been saying to him is in his book. He told me years ago that the Holy Spirit gave him the passage of the Bible, Ezekiel 33:1-21—that is the first part of Ezekiel's call as a watchman. I have no doubt that we are to work together for America as watchmen. I called him about a year ago, and my Bible was opened to Jeremiah 15:15-21. The words were highlighted in a faded yellow, but I did not highlight them. It was the Holy Spirit who did this. There was complete silence. He told me, "I highlighted that passage 30 years ago." It was a sign from the Holy Spirit that we are connected in ministry, and that when the time is right, we are to work together in ministry.

We have to pray for America for some kind of revival. The Bible does say that an even greater falling away will take place (2 Thessalonians 2 KJV). It does not mean that we can't still pray for America. I can see another pandemic coming to America. This may be worse than COVID-19. Let's pray against this—it may just have to take place to awaken the body of Christ. I do not know everything in God's word, and I don't proclaim to. I know there is a dying need for the gospel in America.

I finally realized the Word that the Holy Spirit spoke to me in 2019: "Rebuild walls." God was not speaking of denominations or the church building to be rebuilt. He was talking about people. The walls of the building can be broken down, but the Word of the Lord endures forever (Isaiah 40:8 KJV). I finally realized what the pastor was speaking to me in Colorado in 1992—that I had a calling in my life. For years, I wondered what this calling was, and now I see that ministry is a part of it. My calling is for this book to be sent out into the nations to remind God's people to remain steadfast in the Word.

I have had many dreams since 2020 that will be mentioned later in this book. Let's be obedient and lead people to the Lord. There is power in your testimony—go out and share it with people. What we do in church matters, but what we do outside the walls matters much more. I have so much to say about what God will do for you. He wants you to remain steadfast in His Word and pray for America and the nations. There are millions of Christians in America and throughout the nations. Let's get on our knees like Daniel did and pray for our government. He did not oppose his government; he prayed for them. Prayer can change a lot of things. Obedience is the key to growing in the Lord, and you will mature.

I am writing this to you because I love you, and the Holy Spirit is forever with you. Hallelujah! To God be the glory forever and ever.

How has the Lord spoken to you? Obey Him at all times, and remain in His Word.

Prayer

'Dear heavenly Father, give us the strength to remain steadfast in your Word and to obey You at all times.'

OBEDIENCE

If ye love me, keep my commandments. **John 14:15**

Wherefore gird up the loins of your mind, be sober, and hope to the end for the grace that is to be brought unto you at the revelation of Jesus Christ;

As obedient children, not fashioning yourselves according to the former lusts in your ignorance:

But as he which hath called you is holy, so be ye holy in all manner of conversation;

Because it is written, Be ye holy; for I am holy. **1 Peter 1:13-16**

Then Peter and the other apostles answered and said, We ought to obey God rather than men. **Acts 5:29**

By this, we know that we love the children of God when we love God and keep his commandments.

For this is the love of God, that we keep his commandments: and his commandments are not grievous. **1 John 5:2-3**

If ye be willing and obedient, ye shall eat the good of the land. **Isaiah 1:19**

Now therefore, if ye will obey my voice indeed, and keep my covenant, then ye shall be a peculiar treasure unto me above all people: for all the earth is mine. **Exodus 19:5**

Therefore, thou shalt love the LORD thy God, and keep his charge, and his statutes, and his judgments, and his commandments, always. **Deuteronomy 11:1**

Casting down imaginations, and every high thing that exalteth itself against the knowledge of God, and bringing into captivity every thought to the obedience of Christ;

And having in a readiness to revenge all disobedience, when your obedience is fulfilled. **2 Corinthians 10:5**

Here is the patience of the saints: here are they that keep the commandments of God, and the faith of Jesus. **Revelation 14:12**

By whom we have received grace and apostleship, for obedience to the faith among all nations, for his name. **Romans 10:5**

Ye are my friends, if ye do whatsoever I command you. **John 15:14**

And this is love, that we walk after his commandments. This is the commandment, That, as ye have heard from the beginning, ye should walk in it. **2 John 1:6**

But he said, Yeah rather, blessed are they that hear the word of God,

269

and keep it. **Luke 11:28**

Servants, obey in all things your masters according to the flesh; not with eyeservice, as men-pleasers; but in singleness of heart, fearing God. **Colossians 3:22**

For as by one man's disobedience many were made sinners, so by the obedience of one shall many be made righteous. **Romans 5:19**

Jesus answered and said unto him, If a man loves me, he will keep my words: and my Father will love him, and we will come unto him, and make our abode with him. **John 14:23**

And it shall come to pass, if thou shalt hearken diligently unto the voice of the LORD thy God, to observe and to do all his commandments which I command thee this day, that the LORD thy God will set thee on high above all nations of the earth. **Deuteronomy 28:1**

My son, keep thy father's commandment and forsake not the law of thy mother. **Proverbs 6:20**

But be ye doers of the word, and not hearers only, deceiving your own selves. **James 1:22**

And keep the charge of the LORD thy God, to walk in his ways, to keep his statutes and his commandments, and his judgments, and his testimonies, as it is written in the law of Moses, that thou mayest prosper in all that thou doest, and whithersoever thou turnest thyself. **1 Kings 2:3**

Ye shall walk in all the ways which the LORD your God hath commanded you, that ye may live, and that it may be well with you, and that ye may prolong your days in the land which ye shall possess. **Deuteronomy 5:33**

INTRODUCTION PATIENCE

I lack patience at times, but it is a fruit of the Spirit. God wants us to slow down and know He is God. When we have to wait, it is the Holy Spirit telling us it's all in His time. It took me nearly five years to realize that waiting on the Lord is God's way of shaping us, molding us, and showing us His way, not our own will to be done. My parents became born-again in 1982, and they are still waiting on the Lord for certain areas of ministry.

It took me five years to share my testimony in front of a church body. I was discouraged for a long time, but when I got the opportunity to share my testimony, it was so joyful to share what God was doing in my life. It's all in His time. If you're still waiting, it's because God has a perfect plan for you (Ecclesiastes 3 KJV) and a will for your life. Don't lose hope; He loves you, and His timing for you will come at a perfect time under the sun.

I hope this will encourage you to trust His time and His plan for you. God has not forgotten about you; He will surely do what He has promised to do. The wait, my friend, is hard—I know. We want it to happen right away, but God has you, and He will hold you by your hand and let you know when the time is right. Trust and obey, for there is no other way.

How has waiting on the Lord increased your faith in Jesus to seek

His will and provision for your ministry?

Prayer

'Dear heavenly Father, I know waiting is hard, please be with us while we wait on You, allow us to pray for patience as we wait on You.'

We should always wait for the Lord to show us His way instead of going our own way. Patience is one of the fruits of the Spirit (Galatians 5:22-23). I can recall a time when my patience grew thin. I am the first to admit my patience is thin. Sometimes we need to breathe and let God come in and do the work (Proverbs 14:29). I should have been patient with this person; instead, I let my emotions get in the way. There is nothing the Lord can't handle. We need to rely on His sovereign power, not our own. There is hope for patience (Romans 8:25). With patience, there is hope for God to come in and do the work. Be patient; the Lord will carry you His way and not your own way.

How can we be patient in a busy world?

Prayer

'Heavenly Father, please show us Your love so we can be patient in the things we seek to please You, let us be in Your loving arms and care and guide us in Jesus Christ's name, we pray, Amen.'

PATIENCE

Rejoicing in hope; patient in tribulation; continuing instant in prayer. **Romans 12:12**

I waited patiently for the LORD, and he inclined unto me and heard my cry. **Psalm 40:1**

Be ye also patient; establish your hearts: for the coming of the Lord draweth nigh. **James 5:8**

But if we hope for that we see not, then do we with patience wait for it? **Romans 8:25**

And let us not be weary in well doing: for in due season we shall reap if we faint not. **Galatians 6:9**

For ye have need of patience, that, after ye have done the will of God, ye might receive the promise. **Hebrews 10:36**

Jesus answered and said unto him, What I do thou knowest not now; but thou shalt know hereafter. **John 13:7**

Rest in the LORD, and wait patiently for him: fret not thyself because of him who prospereth in his way, because of the man who bringeth wicked devices to pass. **Psalm 37:7**

Better is the end of a thing than the beginning thereof: and the patient in spirit is better than the proud in spirit. **Ecclesiastes 7:8**

And patience, experience; and experience, hope. **Romans 5:4**

But that on the good ground are they, which in an honest and good heart, having heard the word, keep it, and bring forth fruit with patience. **Luke 8:15**

In your patience possess ye your souls. **Luke 21:19**

But in all things approving ourselves as the ministers of God, in much patience, in afflictions, in necessities, in distresses. **2 Corinthians 6:4**

Strengthened with all might, according to his glorious power, unto all patience and longsuffering with joyfulness. **Colossians 1:11**

Wait on the LORD: be of good courage, and he shall strengthen thine heart: wait, I say, on the LORD. **Psalm 27:14**

INTRODUCTION PURPOSE

We all have a purpose and a plan. It's up to us to pray and seek God to know what His plan is for us. That requires waiting upon the Lord and patience. Trust me, I have been down this road many times. Our plan is not necessarily God's plan. A few years ago, I was swaying to the left and the right, chasing every bit of wind that came around. If it is not God's plan or His will, it will lead to disappointment and failure. His plan and will for you is perfect; it's all in God's timing, my friend.

God has not forgotten about you. You're His child; He has you in the midst of His palms, knitting you together. He has all of His children in His palm. If we have to wait, it's for a reason. Do not get ahead of God. When we do that, it is very dangerous. Always seek His will for you and pray. God has His plans for you. I would not be writing this if He did not have a plan for you. He has a plan for me and every one of His children. It took me nearly five years to discover His purpose for my life and calling. Things will look up for you—I know they will. Allow the Holy Spirit to lead you down His way, to His path.

What is your purpose in life? Has God shown you this plan, or are you still waiting? If you're still waiting, God will continue to guide you.

Prayer

'Heavenly Father, we all have a purpose in life, show Your perfect and pleasing will and the plans You have for us, let us not be discouraged if we have to wait. Loving Father, your plans are much greater than our plans.'

PURPOSE

There are many devices in a man's heart; nevertheless, the counsel of the LORD shall stand. **Proverbs 19:21**

Counsel in the heart of man is like deep water, but a man of understanding will draw it out. **Proverbs 20:5**

The counsel of the LORD standeth forever, the thoughts of his heart to all generations. **Psalm 33:11**

And we know that all things work together for good to them that love God, to them who are the called according to his purpose. **Romans 8:28**

Declaring the end from the beginning and from ancient times the things that are not yet done, saying, My counsel shall stand, and I will do all my pleasure. **Isaiah 46:10**

And in very deed for this cause have I raised thee up, for to shew in thee my power; and that my name may be declared throughout all the earth. **Exodus 9:16**

I know that, whatsoever God doeth, it shall be forever: nothing can be put to it, nor anything taken from it: and God doeth it, that men should fear before him. **Ecclesiastes 3:14**

And I will give them one heart, and one way, that they may fear me forever, for the good of them, and of their children after them. **Jeremiah 32:39**

That they should seek the Lord if haply they might feel after him, and find him, though he is not far from every one of us. **Acts 17:27**

But as we were allowed of God to be put in trust with the gospel, even so, we speak; not as pleasing men, but God, which trieth our hearts. **1 Thessalonians 2:4**

To the intent that now unto the principalities and powers in heavenly places might be known by the church the manifold wisdom of God. **Ephesians 3:10**

I will cry unto God most high; unto God that performeth all things for me. **Psalm 57:2**

The LORD hath made all things for himself: yea, even the wicked for the day of evil. **Proverbs 16:4**

Now I beseech you, brethren, by the name of our Lord Jesus Christ, that ye all speak the same thing, and that there be no divisions among you; but that ye be perfectly joined together in the same mind and in the same judgment. **1 Corinthians 1:10**

Now he that planteth and he that watereth are one: and every man shall receive his own reward according to his own labor. **1 Corinthians 3:8**

I therefore so run, not as uncertainly; so fight I, not as one that beateth the air. **1 Corinthians 9:26**

Only let your conversation be as it becometh the gospel of Christ: that whether I come and see you, or else be absent, I may hear of your affairs, that ye stand fast in one spirit, with one mind striving together for the faith of the gospel. **Philippians 1:27**

Fulfill ye my joy, that ye be likeminded, having the same love, being of one accord, of one mind. **Philippians 2:2**

INTRODUCTION PEACE

Do we have peace within ourselves? Not too long ago, I did not have peace within myself. I did not love myself. I had regrets from before I was serving the Lord, so I looked back at the past. We should not do that; it only brings us down. Look to the present. Are we at peace with ourselves and at peace with people? God wants us to live in total peace; then we will have peace with Him. Jesus said, "Peace I give you, peace I leave with you." God can use us to give others peace as well if we would just sit down and listen to the Holy Spirit. That is all it takes.

We have to have peace; if we don't, our walk with God then becomes distorted. We probably will not hear from God if we do not have peace. Let's be obedient and let the peace that God gives us dwell within our hearts, our homes, and our loved ones. Peace makes the world go around. How can you achieve the peace from God that we are so eagerly desiring? Pray for peace in all areas of your life, and then the peace of God, which surpasses all understanding, will guard your heart and mind in Christ Jesus. My friend, God loves you, and He wants peace to rule over you.

How have you needed peace from God in your life to overcome difficult struggles?

Prayer

'Dear heavenly Father, please give us the peace that we desire that will rule in our heart to overcome the enemy and move forward in our walk with God.'

PEACE

These things I have spoken unto you, that in me ye might have peace. In the world ye shall have tribulation: but be of good cheer; I have overcome the world. **John 16:33**

Blessed are the peacemakers: for they shall be called the children of God. **Matthew 5:9**

Let him eschew evil, and do good; let him seek peace, and ensue it. **1 Peter 3:11**

I will both lay me down in peace, and sleep: for thou, LORD, only makest me dwell in safety. **Psalm 4:8**

Peace I leave with you, my peace I give unto you: not as the world giveth, give I unto you. Let not your heart be troubled, neither let it be afraid. **John 14:27**

And the fruit of righteousness is sown in peace of them that make peace. **James 3:18**

Depart from evil, and do good; seek peace, and pursue it. **Psalms 34:14**

Endeavoring to keep the unity of the Spirit in the bond of peace. **Ephesians 4:3**

Great peace have they which love thy law: and nothing shall offend them. **Psalm 119:165**

Those things, which ye have both learned, and received, and heard, and seen in me, do: and the God of peace shall be with you. **Philippians 4:9**

For to be carnally minded is death, but to be spiritually minded is life and peace. **Romans 8:6**

How beautiful upon the mountains are the feet of him that bringeth good tidings, that publisheth peace; that bringeth good tidings of good, that publisheth salvation; that saith unto Zion, Thy God reigneth! **Isaiah 52:7**

If it be possible, as much as lieth in you, live peaceably with all men. **Romans 12:18**

Finally, brethren, farewell. Be perfect, be of good comfort, be of one mind, live in peace; and the God of love and peace shall be with you. **2 Corinthians 13:11**

My son, forget not my law; but let thine heart keep my commandments:

For length of days, and long life, and peace, shall they add to thee. **Proverbs 3:1-2**

Then said Jesus to them again, Peace be unto you: as my Father hath sent me, even so send I you. **John 20:21**

Now the God of peace, that brought again from the dead our Lord Jesus, that great shepherd of the sheep, through the blood of the everlasting covenant,

Make you perfect in every good work to do his will, working in you that which is well pleasing in his sight, through Jesus Christ; to who be glory forever and ever. Amen. **Hebrews 13:20-21**

And the God of peace shall bruise Satan under your feet shortly. The grace of our Lord Jesus Christ is with you. Amen. **Romans 16:20**

And the man wondering at her held his peace, to wit whether the LORD had made his journey prosperous or not. **Genesis 24:21**

Acquaint now thyself with him, and be at peace: thereby good shall come unto thee. **Job 22:21**

Now the God of peace be with you all. Amen. **Romans 15:33**

And to esteem them very highly in love for their work's sake. And be at peace among yourselves. **1 Thessalonians 15:33**

They say still unto them that despise me, The LORD hath said, Ye shall have peace; and they say unto every one that walketh after the

imagination of his own heart, No evil shall come upon you.
Jeremiah 23:17

INTRODUCTION PROTECTION

God protects His people from potential harm. His protection is upon us when we pray to Him. I wake up every morning and plead the blood of Jesus over my life, my son, my house, and my family. When we do this, God sends His angels to watch over us. When you get into your car to drive, pray over your vehicle for Jesus' blood to keep you safe and for the enemy to be far away from your camp. I do this every time before I get into my vehicle.

On November 25, 2022, my life flashed before my eyes. I was driving to go Black Friday shopping, and a truck pulled out in front of me. I was driving at speeds of 55 miles per hour. The driver T-boned me. It happened so fast that I had no time to slam on my brakes. Once I realized what had happened, I looked over at my son for a second. He was not breathing. I screamed, "No, God, no! Please don't take him away from me. He is all I have." He then started breathing. The first responders came, and so did all the rest of the law enforcement. They looked at both vehicles and told us, "You're blessed. It could have been worse. An accident like this usually results in people losing their lives." My son broke his collarbone. God was with us, and the driver of the truck. God's angels were in our vehicle, protecting us and our vehicle. We should have died. God's purpose for my life is far greater than Satan's schemes. This accident happened just two weeks before I was going to leave for Africa. Satan knew God was going to use my mother and me mightily, and he tried to stop it. God wasn't going to allow this to happen. He has a plan for me and you. I am blessed. The accident could have been worse. Always pray for protection over your life.

How has praying for protection saved you from harm and danger from the enemy?

Prayer

'Loving Father, we pray for protection over our lives, keep the enemy far away from us, we rebuke any kind of schemes that Satan is trying to do.'

PROTECTION

No weapon that is formed against thee shall prosper; and every tongue that shall rise against thee in judgment thou shalt condemn. This is the heritage of the servants of the LORD, and their righteousness is of me, saith the LORD. **Isaiah 54:17**

But the Lord is faithful, who shall establish you, and keep you from evil. **2 Thessalonians 3:3**

Thou art my hiding place; thou shalt preserve me from trouble; thou shalt compass me about with songs of deliverance. **Psalm 32:7**

Thou art my hiding place and my shield: I hope in thy word. **Psalm 119:114**

But let all those that put their trust in thee rejoice: let them ever shout for joy because thou defendest them: let them also that love thy name be joyful in thee. **Psalm 5:11**

For the oppression of the poor, for the sighing of the needy, now will I arise, saith the LORD; I will set him in safety from him that puffeth at him. **Psalm 12:5**

Deliver me from mine enemies, O my God: defend me from them that rise up against me. **Psalm 59:1**

Though I walk in the midst of trouble, thou wilt revive me: thou shalt stretch forth thine hand against the wrath of mine enemies, and thy right hand shall save me. **Psalm 138:7**

Keep me, O LORD, from the hands of the wicked; preserve me from the violent man; who have purposed to overthrow my goings. **Psalms 140:4**

Many are the afflictions of the righteous: but the LORD delivereth him out of them all. **Psalm 34:19**

The God of my rock; in him will I trust: he is my shield, and the horn of my salvation, my high tower, and my refuge, my savior; thou savest me from violence.

I will call on the LORD, who is worthy to be praised: so shall I be saved from mine enemies. **2 Samuel 22:3-4**

And the Lord shall deliver me from every evil work and will preserve me unto his heavenly kingdom: to whom be glory forever and ever. Amen. **2 Timothy 4:18**

INTRODUCTION PRAYER

Prayer is very important in our daily lives. Take time to spend with the Lord and pray; He hears us. Prayer changes everything. I recall a situation where the Lord answered my prayer. I was at a job I had just been hired for. I was there for about two months and was not catching on in the department I was placed in. I am a slow learner. I was praying to the Lord for favor at my job. I did everything they asked me to do and was afraid they were going to let me go.

One day at work, my supervisor came to me and said, "Hey Joshua, I need to talk to you." I thought, "This is it; I am going to be let go." He said, "Don't worry; we are not going to let you go. We see that you are a dedicated employee. I have talked to our plant manager, and you're not catching on to what you are doing, so we are going to place you in a different department." I was so joyful; my spirit was lifted high because God had heard my prayer and answered it.

Don't get discouraged if God does not answer your prayers right away; it's all in His time. Go to your quarters and pray (Matthew 6:9-13 KJV). Prayer can change the atmosphere. Pray for your loved ones, pray for those who persecute you and use you (Matthew 5:44 KJV), and pray for America and the nations. God is a very loving God; He can change His mind. Pray for our nations to repent and turn away from wickedness. Pray in the Spirit; He hears us and will answer us. To God be the glory.

How has praying lifted you up and others? How has God come through and answered your prayers?

Prayer

'Loving Father, we pray to You many times to keep our focus on You, so we are not distracted from praying. We fix our eyes on You, Father, and pray for our nations and families, and friends to come into a relationship with You.'

PRAYER

Hear me when I call, O God of my righteousness: thou hast enlarged me when I was in distress; have mercy upon me, and hear my prayer. **Psalms 4:1**

For this shall everyone that is Godly pray unto thee in a time when thou mayest be found: surely in the floods of great waters they shall not come nigh unto him. **Psalms 32:6**

Hear my prayer, O LORD, and give ear unto my cry; hold not thy peace at my tears: for I am a stranger with thee, and a sojourner, as all my fathers were. **Psalms 39:12**

But verily God hath heard me; he hath attended to the voice of my prayer. **Psalms 66:19**

Thou shalt make thy prayer unto him, and he shall hear thee, and thou shalt pay thy vows. **Job 22:27**

The LORD is far from the wicked: but he heareth the prayer of the righteous. **Proverbs 15:29**

Now therefore, O our God, hear the prayer of thy servant, and his supplications, and cause thy face to shine upon thy sanctuary that is desolate, for the Lord's sake. **Daniel 9:17**

When my soul fainted within me, I remembered the LORD: and my prayer came in unto thee, into thine holy temple. **Jonah 2:7**

Therefore, I say unto you, What things soever ye desire when ye pray, believe that ye receive them, and ye shall have them. **Mark 11:24**

Likewise, the Spirit also helpeth our infirmities: for we know not what we should pray for as we ought: but the Spirit itself maketh intercession for us with groanings which cannot be uttered. **Romans 8:26**

Continue in prayer, and watch in the same with thanksgiving. **Colossians 4:2**

Praying always with all prayer and supplication in the Spirit, and watching thereunto with all perseverance and supplication for all saints. **Ephesians 6:18**

Rejoice evermore.

Pray without ceasing.

In everything give thanks: for this is the will of God in Christ Jesus concerning you. **1 Thessalonians 5:16-18**

And I say unto you, Ask, and it shall be given you; seek, and ye shall find; knock, and it shall be opened unto you. **Luke 11:9**

Confess your faults one to another, and pray one for another, that ye may be healed. The effectual fervent prayer of a righteous man availeth much. **James 5:16**

Evening, and morning, and at noon, will I pray, and cry aloud: and he shall hear my voice. **Psalms 55:12**

But your iniquities have separated between you and your God, and your sins have hidden his face from you, that he will not hear. **Isaiah 59:2**

And when ye spread forth your hands, I will hide mine eyes from you: yea, when ye make many prayers, I will not hear: your hands are full of blood. **Isaiah 1:15**

INTRODUCTION PATH

What path are you on, and which paths has God told us to get off? I have been down many roads and paths. The path that you are on might not necessarily be God's path. I knew a certain path I was going to go on; God told me, "This is not the way I want you to go."

I had a date in March of 2022. We went to a wild game feast. The night was very nice; we had a great time. The wild game feast was put on by a Christian evangelist who was a hunter. He had hunted around the world and gave a great speech about how God changed his life. As the night progressed, I was interested in seeing her again. When the night was over, we agreed to meet up again sometime.

That night, I went home and had a very intense dream. I was in a shopping mall, and a man came up to me. He started yelling at me, "That's my wife," and pointed at a lady. The lady he pointed at was the woman I had just gone on a date with. After that, I woke up. I asked God, "Was this from You or Satan?"

The next day, I called her and asked, "Are you married?" She said no. I went to work the next day and texted her, "I really like you, but I am putting God first. My son and my studies are important to me. If this leads to anything else, like more dating, that's awesome. God is number one in my life." She then blocked me.

After that, I wondered about my dream. I did a social media search and looked at her profile. It turns out the man in my dream who told me she was his wife was indeed her husband. I was blown away. Had I chosen to continue on that path, it would have led to destruction. It was the Holy Spirit working in the supernatural to keep me safe.

If we are open to the Holy Spirit, we are also open to Satan. He can come as an angel of light. He can speak to us, "Oh, you want to go on this path; this is the way to go. You will have major success." Satan wants to destroy us; he wants us to fail. If I had gone down that road, I would have failed. We have to be able to discern, "Is this God's voice or Satan's voice?" He can speak to us just like God can. If Satan can try to test Jesus, he will tempt us (Matthew 4:1-11 KJV). The path that God wants us on will be evident; it will be clear.

What path are you on, and what path do you need to get off? Ask Jesus, and He will show you which path to take.

Prayer

'Heavenly Father, show us Your perfect path, be the center of our path so we know which path we need to take and which path to get off.'

PATH

The paths of their way are turned aside; they go to nothing and perish. **Job 6:18**

Concerning the works of men, by the word of thy lips I have kept me from the paths of the destroyer.

Hold up my goings in thy paths, that my footsteps slip not. **Psalm 17:4- 5**

Shew me thy ways, O LORD; teach me thy paths. **Psalm 25:4**

And I will bring the blind by a way that they knew not; I will lead them in paths that they have not known: I will make darkness light before them, and crooked things straight. These things will I do unto them, and not forsake them. **Isaiah 42:16**

Who leave the paths of uprightness, to walk in the ways of darkness. **Proverbs 2:13**

And many people shall go and say, Come ye, and let us go up to the mountain of the LORD, to the house of the God of Jacob; and he will teach us of his ways, and we will walk in his paths: for out of Zion shall go forth the law, and the word of the LORD from Jerusalem. **Isaiah 2:3**

Therefore, behold, I will hedge up thy way with thorns, and make a wall, that she shall not find her paths. **Hosea 2:6**

The voice of one crying in the wilderness, Prepare ye the way of the Lord, make his paths straight. **Mark 1:3**

As it is written in the book of the words of Esaias the prophet, saying, The voice of one crying in the wilderness, Prepare ye the way of the Lord, make his paths straight. **Luke 3:4**

And make straight paths for your feet, lest that which is lame be turned out of the way; but let it rather be healed. **Hebrews 12:13**

Thy word is a lamp unto my feet and a light unto my path. **Psalm 119:105**

Ponder the path of thy feet, and let all thy ways be established. **Proverbs 4:26**

Thou hast enlarged my steps under me, that my feet did not slip. **Psalm 18:36**

There is a way which seemeth right unto a man, but the end thereof are the ways of death. **Proverbs 14:12**

Trust in the LORD with all thine heart; and lean not unto thine own understanding.

In all thy ways acknowledge him, and he shall direct thy paths. **Proverbs 3:5-6**

Thus, saith the LORD, Stand ye in the ways, and see, and ask for the old paths, where is the good way, and walk therein, and ye shall find rest for your souls. But they said We will not walk therein. **Jeremiah 6:16**

Her ways are ways of pleasantness, and all her paths are peace. **Proverbs 3:17**

So are the paths of all that forget God; and the hypocrite's hope shall perish. **Job 8:13**

He putteth my feet in the stocks, he marketh all my paths. **Job 33:11**

None that go unto her return again, neither take they hold of the paths of life.

That thou mayest walk in the way of good men, and keep the paths of the righteous. **Proverbs 2:19-20**

Let not thine heart decline to her ways, go not astray in her paths. **Proverbs 7:25**

INTRODUCTION PRAISE AND WORSHIP

Our praise and worship should be glorious. It is our form of thanking God for what He has done. We shall worship our God in spirit and in truth. Praise and worship are not just jumping up and down and raising hands and arms in the air. The Bible does say to raise hands in the sanctuary (Psalm 134:2 KJV), and some people do that. However, some people have a quiet spirit, and that is okay. How do you praise and worship God?

I do raise my hands and worship Jesus for what He has done. Some people don't do that, and that's fine. The Bible does say that our worship should be glorious, shouting to the heavens how majestic His name is in all of the earth. Should we raise our hands? I think we should, but that is just my kind of worship. To dance with joy, how wonderful our Savior is! When we worship like the angels and the saints who have gone before us, we honor God deeply.

I went to the altar on Pentecost Sunday in May of 2023. I was giving God thanks for what He has done for me. I was in tune and in oneness with the Holy Spirit. I had a vision of a dove flying around me. It flew around me three times and then went into my body, into my spirit. I could feel a fresh fire and electricity going through my body. It was amazing to experience this. That is what worship is about.

It does not matter what other people think of us; worship how you want to worship. I'm sure some of you have had an experience like I did with the dove flying into me. If you have, who was it? The Holy Spirit told me who it was. His Words were powerful. When He laid His hands on me, I could feel more fire and more electricity coming out of Him and into me. It was awesome to experience this.

A week later, God told me to prophesy over Him: "You have a calling and a gift that you don't know you have. You're a prayer warrior, and God wants you to fully surrender to what He wants you to do." What an awesome week that was! That's true worship—when we go to the altar to submit and surrender to His will.

How is your praise and worship in church? Can we do more to glorify the Lord?

Prayer

'Dear heavenly Father, I come boldly to your throne of grace. I ask you, Father, to do good work in your church, to bring back that fire and praise worship with people surrendering all they have to offer you. Loving gracious Father, bring back that old-time praise and worship like it was back in the early church, I ask you, Father, to restore your true praise and worship back to your church in Jesus Christ's name, I pray, Amen.'

God wants us to praise Him and worship Him; it's a vital part of our faith to worship Him in spirit and in truth (John 4:24). Worship brings us closer to God. I encourage you to worship the Lord with everything we have to offer Him. Praise Him for what He has done in our lives.

Should praise and worship be done only while we are at church? Absolutely not. We are to worship and praise God wherever we are— whether we are at home, in public, or at church. Remember, worship and praise are not just about dancing, lifting your hands up, and jumping around. It's about who He is and what He has done for us. It brings us closer to the Lord when we praise Him.

Not everyone has the same spirit when they worship and praise. Some may dance and lift their hands up to the Lord, while others have a quiet spirit. We should not look down on people who don't raise their hands. God's Word says, "Draw near to Me, and I will draw near to you" (James 4:8). When we worship and praise, God speaks to us and gives us words of encouragement. He is worthy of our praise. To God be the glory!

How can we praise and worship to draw near to God? Scripture reference

Psalm 150:1-6

Psalm 66:1

1 Chronicles 16:29

Prayer

'Loving Father, thank you for what You did for us by giving Your life for us. We ask you, Father, to be in the midst of our life to worship and praise You for who You are. Please, Father, continue to draw near to us as we draw near to You in Jesus Christ's name, we pray, Amen.'

PRAISE AND WORSHIP

God is a Spirit: and they who worship him must worship him in spirit and in truth. **John 4:24**

O come, let us worship and bow down: let us kneel before the LORD our maker. **Psalms 95:6**

I beseech you therefore, brethren, by the mercies of God, that ye present your bodies a living sacrifice, holy, acceptable unto God, which is your reasonable service. **Romans 12:1**

He is thy praise, and he is thy God, that hath done for thee these great and terrible things, which thine eyes have seen. **Deuteronomy 10:21**

Sing unto the LORD, praise ye the LORD: for he hath delivered the soul of the poor from the hand of evildoers. **Jeremiah 20:13**

Unto thee, O God, do we give thanks, unto thee do we give thanks: for that thy name is near thy wondrous works declare. **Psalm 75:1**

And Jesus answered and said unto him, Get thee behind me, Satan: for it is written, Thou shalt worship the Lord thy God, and him only shalt thou serve. **Luke 4:8**

I will be glad and rejoice in thee: I will sing praise to thy name, O thou most High. **Psalm 9:2**

Because thy lovingkindness is better than life, my lips shall praise thee.

Thus, will I bless thee while I live: I will lift up my hands in thy name. **Psalm 63:3-4**

Praise ye the LORD. Praise God in his sanctuary: praise him in the firmament of his power.

Praise him for his mighty acts: praise him according to his excellent greatness.

Praise him with the sound of the trumpet: praise him with the psaltery and harp.

Praise him with the timbrel and dance: praise him with stringed instruments and organs.

Praise him upon the loud cymbals: praise him upon the high-sounding cymbals.

Let everything that hath breath praise the LORD. Praise ye the LORD. **Psalm 150:1-6**

Make a joyful noise unto the LORD, all ye lands. **Psalm 100:1**

Enter into his gates with thanksgiving, and into his courts with praise: be thankful unto him, and bless his name. **Psalm 100:4**

I will extol thee, my God, O king; and I will bless thy name forever and ever.

Every day will I bless thee, and I will praise thy name forever and ever.

Great is the LORD, and greatly to be praised, and his greatness is unsearchable. **Psalm 145:1-3**

Let my mouth be filled with thy praise and with thy honor all the day. **Psalm 71:8**

Let the word of Christ dwell in you richly in all wisdom; teaching and admonishing one another in psalms and hymns and spiritual songs, singing with grace in your hearts to the Lord. **Colossians 3:16**

Sing unto God, sing praises to his name: extol him that rideth upon the heavens by his name JAH, and rejoice before him. **Psalm 68:4**

Bless the LORD, O my soul: and all that is within me, bless his holy name. **Psalm 103:1**

Sing praises to the LORD, which dwelleth in Zion: declare among the people his doings. Psalm 9:11 I will praise thee, O LORD, among the people: and I will sing praises unto thee among the nations. **Psalm 108:3**

I will praise thee with uprightness of heart when I shall have learned thy righteous judgments. **Psalm 119:7**

INTRODUCTION PRIDE

Pride will lead to destruction. We all have a little pride in us—pride in our work, pride in our children—and there is nothing wrong with that. I am talking about the pride that we let settle in for the ministry that God has given us. Once we take credit for what God is doing in our lives and ministry, it leads to pride. Trust me, I have seen a lot of that in the past five years that I have been doing this. It becomes too much focus on ourselves.

What happened to Satan when he tried to overtake the throne of God? He was cast out of heaven. That should be a lesson for us. Once we become prideful in our ministry, the Lord could take it away from us, just like He kicked Satan out of heaven. I became prideful a few years back. At a retreat I am involved with, I gave a talk in the conference room in October of 2022. My talk was amazing, but I used that for my glory and did not give God much credit. I called a friend a few weeks later after my talk, and he told me, "Is it God that did the talk, or you?" Those words hit me like a ton of bricks. I said it was God. He reminded me to stay humble. God will nudge us when we become prideful, or He can use people, as in this case, my friend.

I can become self-centered at times. The Lord brings me back to reality, back to being humble. The proud will get setbacks from the

Lord. Look what happened to Moses—he saw the promised land but did not get to go into the land because of his pride. He said, "I am going to strike the rock." It was his pride; he did not acknowledge the Lord, that it was He doing the work. Water still came out, but his pride was a stumbling block. Do not let pride overtake you, or you will not see the blessings the Lord has in store for you. The Holy Spirit will help you through this so that pride will not become an issue. I ask myself a question: Did this bring me glory, or did it bring God glory?

How has pride been a stumbling block in your ministry, and how can we let go of this?

Prayer

'Dear heavenly Father, I pray that we can let go of pride and brag about You and not ourselves. I ask you, Father, to show us what we need to work on and let go of, so we can have more of You and less of ourselves. It's you doing the work, not us. In Jesus Christ's name, we pray, Amen.'

PRIDE

When pride cometh, then cometh shame: but with the lowly is wisdom. **Proverbs 11:2**

Everyone that is proud in heart is an abomination to the LORD: though hand joins in hand, he shall not be unpunished. **Proverbs 16:5**

A man's pride shall bring him low: but honor shall uphold the humble in spirit. **Proverbs 29:23**

Pride goeth before destruction and a haughty spirit before a fall. **Proverbs 16:18**

Seest thou a man wise in his own conceit? there is more hope of a fool than of him. **Proverbs 26:12**

Let nothing be done through strife or vainglory, but in lowliness of mind let each esteem other better than themselves. **Philippians 2:3**

The fear of the LORD is to hate evil: pride, and arrogancy, and the evil way, and the froward mouth, do I hate. **Proverbs 8:13**

But he giveth more grace. Wherefore he saith, God resisteth the proud, but giveth grace unto the humble. **James 4:6**

Thus, saith the LORD, Let not the wise man glory in his wisdom, neither let the mighty man glory in his might, let not the rich man glory in his riches. **Jeremiah 9:23**

For all that is in the world, the lust of the flesh, and the lust of the eyes, and the pride of life, is not of the Father but is of the world. **1 John 2:16**

Be of the same mind one toward another. Mind not high things, but condescend to men of low estate. Be not wise in your own conceits. **Romans 12:16**

For I say, through the grace given unto me, to every man that is among you, not to think of himself more highly than he ought to think, but to think soberly, according as God hath dealt to every man the measure of faith. **Romans 12:3**

For if a man thinks himself to be something, when he is nothing, he deceiveth himself.

But let every man prove his own work, and then shall he have rejoicing in himself alone, and not in another.

For every man shall bear his own burden. **Galatians 6:3-5**

PATH LEAD TO SUCCESS

The path that we are on can lead to either failure or success in every situation or decision, like a job change, buying a house, purchasing a car, etc. We should always ask God first. I can recall a time when I needed advice, but I went to everyone else instead of going to God first. I wanted it my way, but our way leads to failure, maybe even depression. We should rely on the Holy Spirit and pray continually (1 Thessalonians 5:16-19).

When we hit that T-intersection, what do we do? We can't go straight anymore; we have to make a decision. It's God's way of directing our path. We should pray and seek God first. Commit to the Lord whatever we do, and our plans will be established (Proverbs 16:3).

I encourage you to let the Holy Spirit be your guide to the path you need to be on. Allow God to be the center of your path; He will guide your every step. Your path will determine your future. Learn how to trust the Lord, and He will give you understanding and peace with the path that you are on.

How can we rely on the Holy Spirit to guide our path to Victory?

Prayer

'Dear heavenly Father, please guide my every step to be on the path that You want me on, I will trust You, Lord, with my life.'

INTRODUCTION REPENTANCE

If we truly love God, repenting of our sins is easy. God wants us to always repent when we sin; He washes us clean every time. His blood was shed for us to cover our sins. We should do our best to avoid sin when it comes our way, and it will. Allow the Holy Spirit to teach you to live a godly life so that you don't want to sin. When we do sin, it separates us from God, and we cannot condone sin. When we do this, God is displeased.

At the end of the day, ask God to forgive you for the sins you commit, even for the sins you have no idea you committed. God loves you, and He wants to teach us to repent. I have committed many sins. I always ask my loving Father for His forgiveness, and He washes us clean.

When in a time in your life did you had to ask God to forgive you?

Prayer

'Heavenly Father, please remain in us so we don't want to sin when it comes our way, we ask You to be the center of our life to run away from sin.'

REPENTANCE

And saying, Repent ye: for the kingdom of heaven is at hand. **Matthew 3:2**

Bring forth therefore fruits meet for repentance. **Matthew 3:8**

Repent ye therefore, and be converted, that your sins may be blotted out when the times of refreshing shall come from the presence of the Lord. **Acts 3:19**

Now I rejoice, not that ye were made sorry, but that ye sorrowed to repentance: for ye were made sorry after a Godly manner, that ye might receive damage by us in nothing.

For Godly sorrow worketh repentance to salvation not to be repented of: but the sorrow of the world worketh death. **2 Corinthians 7:9-10**

The Lord is not slack concerning his promise, as some men count slackness; but is longsuffering to us-ward, not willing that any should perish, but that all should come to repentance. **2 Peter 3:9**

From that time Jesus began to preach, and to say, Repent: for the kingdom of heaven is at hand. **Matthew 4:17**

Then Peter said unto them, Repent, and be baptized every one of you in the name of Jesus Christ for the remission of sins, and ye shall receive the gift of the Holy Ghost. **Acts 2:38**

And the times of this ignorance God winked at, but now commandeth all men everywhere to repent. **Acts 17:30**

Or despisest thou the riches of his goodness and forbearance and longsuffering; not knowing that the goodness of God leadeth thee to repentance? **Romans 2:4**

If my people, which are called by my name, shall humble themselves, and pray, and seek my face, and turn from their wicked ways; then will I hear from heaven, and will forgive their sin, and will heal their land. **2 Chronicles 7:14**

When they heard these things, they held their peace, and glorified God, saying, Then hath God also to the Gentiles granted repentance unto life. **Acts 11:18**

I tell you, Nay: but, except ye repent, ye shall all likewise perish. **Luke 13:3**

In meekness instructing those that oppose themselves; if God peradventure will give them repentance to the acknowledging of the truth. **2 Timothy 2:25**

As many as I love, I rebuke and chasten: be zealous, therefore, and repent. **Revelation 3:19**

And rend your heart, and not your garments, and turn unto the LORD your God: for he is gracious and merciful, slow to anger, and of great kindness, and repenteth him of the evil. **Joel 2:13**

Therefore, say thou unto them, Thus saith the LORD of hosts; Turn ye unto me, saith the LORD of hosts, and I will turn unto you, saith the LORD of hosts. **Zechariah 1:3**

REJECTION

In our walk with Jesus, we will have people who reject us. That's okay—remember, the Pharisees rejected Jesus. In our lives, rejection sometimes happens. Have you been recently rejected by someone, such as a friend, coworker, family member, or someone at church? It's a part of life to be rejected. Does it hurt? Of course, it does. I have been rejected a lot in my life, and it still happens from time to time. If we are saved and belong to Jesus, we will be rejected, but the Lord will never reject us (Psalm 27:8-11). We are His prized possession, and He will never fail us.

When we are rejected, we can go to Jesus and pray. The Scriptures will help us get through this. God loves you; He has you. When I was young, the rejection really hurt me, but just think of the rejection Jesus took, and He still loved the people. Religion is what killed Jesus. If He was rejected, we will be too (Isaiah 53:3). Trust the Holy Spirit to help you through your pain when people reject you. The Lord is good; He will never reject you. Once you're saved, you're in His arms.

When you're down, do not be discouraged or feel like you're not good enough. It's the devil's tactic to get into our minds. Rejection happens, and we have to learn how to cope with it. The Holy Spirit is the ultimate gentleman; He loves you, and you're His child. All we

319

have to do is remember what He did for us on an old rugged cross and how He gave His life for us. He was rejected, and He had to suffer. We will have pains and sorrows just like Jesus did. We are overcomers, and God has you in the midst of His palms. So, when we are rejected, we can go to Jesus in prayer and petition. He will comfort us in times of rejection, knowing He is Lord and Savior.

How does rejection affect you? Have you been recently rejected? How can we handle this when rejection arises?

Prayer

'Lord Jesus, please, when we are rejected, be with us and help us through this; there is nothing You can't do to help us overcome rejection. You overcame death and rejection and gave us eternal life. Help us, Father, to get through the difficult times in our lives. In Jesus Christ's name, we pray, Amen.'

RESISTING TEMPTATION

Some days are more challenging than others. We all go through various ordeals in life that will either bring us closer to God or lead us into temptation, giving birth to sin, and allowing the enemy to come in to kill, steal, and destroy (John 10:10). My friend, God does not tempt us—the devil does. Be extra careful and cautious in every situation we go through. When we are tempted, God's Word gives us a way of escape (1 Corinthians 10:13). Avoid all temptation. Satan wants us to give in, and this draws us further away from God. When we fail to notice the signs that the Holy Spirit uses for us to flee temptation, we eventually give in to sin. In other words, sin is born within us. Stay on track: read the Bible, go to church, pray, fast, be in fellowship with other believers, be on your guard, and resist the devil. When we flee from temptation, we have stood the test and received the crown of life that the Lord has promised to those who love Him (James 1:12). We love God, and God loves us. If we flee from temptation, we become stronger in our faith, and our faith in the Lord gives us eternal life, which will never fade away (Isaiah 40:8). God loves you, my friend, and He will see you through any trial or temptation.

In what ways can we experience temptation, and how can we avoid it?

Prayer

'Heavenly Father, please be with us in every situation that could lead us into temptation, please Lord give us a way out as we continue to serve You in our life, we put our trust and hope in You. In Jesus Christ's name, we pray, Amen.'

INTRODUCTION STRENGTH

God gives us the strength to move forward. His power can help us stay focused on the Holy Spirit in a busy and difficult world. Our strength can wear us down at times, but the Holy Spirit can help us as we become weak. He carries us in His power, not in our own power and strength. When we rely on our own strength, it leads to disappointment and failure. We need to remain focused on Jesus and rely on His strength, not our own (John 15:5). When we rely on Jesus, we bear fruit. Many times, I have become weak and tired, but the Holy Spirit lifts us up, and then His strength becomes our victory. There is power in the blood of the Lamb to overcome our weakness; then His strength becomes the Holy Spirit's power. Rely on God's strength, not ours. The Holy Spirit will show you the way to go and turn, so we are not relying on man's power. My friend, God will help you on your journey.

How has God's power and strength working in you helped you, and how did using your strength turn out? Let's keep focused on the Holy Spirit's power.

Prayer

'Dear Heavenly Father, work in us and through us so that we rely on your strength and not our own. Please remain with us so we are always focused on you and using your strength, when we start using our strength, show us to rely on you at all times.'

STRENGTH

My flesh and my heart faileth: but God is the strength of my heart, and my portion forever. **Psalm 73:26**

Then he said unto them, Go your way, eat the fat, and drink the sweet, and send portions unto them for whom nothing is prepared: for this day is holy unto our LORD: neither be ye sorry; for the joy of the LORD is your strength. **Nehemiah 8:10**

I can do all things through Christ which strengtheneth me. **Philippians 4:13**

O God, thou art terrible out of thy holy places: the God of Israel is he that giveth strength and power unto his people. Blessed be God. **Psalms 68:35**

My soul melteth for heaviness: strengthen thou me according unto thy word. **Psalm 119:28**

The LORD is my strength and my shield; my heart trusted in him, and I am helped: therefore, my heart greatly rejoiceth; and with my song will I praise him. **Psalms 28:7**

Strength and honor are her clothing, and she shall rejoice in time to come. **Proverbs 31:25**

The LORD is my strength and song, and he has become my salvation: he is my God, and I will prepare him in habitation; my father's God, and I will exalt him. **Exodus 15:2**

Behold, God is my salvation; I will trust, and not be afraid: for the LORD, JEHOVAH is my strength and my song; he also is become my salvation. **Isaiah 12:2**

He giveth power to the faint; and to them that have no might he increaseth strength. **Isaiah 40:29**

But the God of all grace, who hath called us unto his eternal glory by Christ Jesus, after that ye have suffered a while, make you perfect, stablish, strengthen, settle you. **1 peter 5:10**

And he said unto me, My grace is sufficient for thee: for my strength is made perfect in weakness. Most gladly therefore will I rather glory in my infirmities, that the power of Christ may rest upon me.

Therefore, I take pleasure in infirmities, in reproaches, in necessities, in persecutions, in distresses for Christ's sake: for when I am weak, then am I strong. **2 Corinthians 12:9-10**

God is our refuge and strength, a very present help in trouble. **Psalm 46:1**

But they that wait upon the LORD shall renew their strength; they shall mount up with wings as eagles; they shall run, and not be weary; and they shall walk, and not faint. **Isaiah 40:31**

I will love thee, O LORD, my strength.

The LORD is my rock, and my fortress, and my deliverer; my God, my strength, in whom I will trust; my buckler, and the horn of my salvation, and my high tower. **Psalm 18:1-2**

The LORD God is my strength, and he will make my feet like hinds' feet, and he will make me walk upon mine high places. To the chief singer on my stringed instruments. **Habakkuk 3:19**

INTRODUCTION SALVATION

There is only one way to heaven, and it's not by going to church or doing good works. We could go to church for 50-plus years, but if we don't have a relationship with Jesus, it's all for nothing. The only way to enter heaven is to repent, ask for forgiveness, repent of our sins, and invite Jesus to come into our hearts and lives. It has to be a heartfelt prayer, such as this:

"Dear Heavenly Father, please forgive me of my sins. I repent, ask for Your forgiveness, and turn away from wickedness. I invite You to come into my heart to be Lord of my life."

My friend, this is the only way to heaven. Once you have done this, you belong to the family of God, and your name is now registered in the Book of Life.

Do you remember the day you were saved, and how it was? I remember the day I was truly saved; it was amazing.

Prayer

'Heavenly Father, please continue to keep us on track and use us to lead others to you. May your love bubble to others through us.'

SALVATION

Neither is there salvation in any other: for there is none other name under heaven given among men, whereby we must be saved. **Acts 4:12**

Jesus saith unto him, I am the way, the truth, and the life: no man cometh unto the Father but by me. **John 14:6**

Not by works of righteousness which we have done, but according to his mercy he saved us, by the washing of regeneration, and renewing of the Holy Ghost. **Titus 3:5**

For God so loved the world, that he gave his only begotten Son, that whosoever believeth in him should not perish, but have everlasting life. **John 3:16**

And brought them out, and said, Sirs, what must I do to be saved?

And they said, Believe on the Lord Jesus Christ, and thou shalt be saved, and thy house. **Acts 16:30-31**

That if thou shalt confess with thy mouth the Lord Jesus, and shalt believe in thine heart that God hath raised him from the dead, thou shalt be saved.

For with the heart, man believeth unto righteousness, and with the mouth, confession is made unto salvation. **Romans 10:9-10**

Wherefore he is able also to save them to the uttermost that come unto God by him, seeing he ever liveth to make intercession for them. **Hebrews 7:25**

And the Spirit and the bride say, Come. And let him that heareth say, Come. And let him that is athirst come. And whosoever will, let him take the water of life freely. **Revelation 22:17**

Wherefore, my beloved, as ye have always obeyed, not as in my presence only, but now much more in my absence, work out your own salvation with fear and trembling.

For it is God which worketh in you both to will and to do of his good pleasure. **Philippians 2:12-13**

But as many as received him, to them he gave power to become the sons of God, even to them that believe in his name:

Which were born, not of blood, nor of the will of the flesh, nor of the will of man, but of God. **John 1:12-13**

In whom ye also trusted, after that ye heard the word of truth, the gospel of your salvation: in whom also, after that ye believed, ye were sealed with that holy Spirit of promise,

Which is the earnest of our inheritance until the redemption of the purchased possession, unto the praise of his glory. **Ephesians 1:13-14**

Jesus answered and said unto him, Verily, verily, I say unto thee, Except a man be born again, he cannot see the kingdom of God.

Nicodemus saith unto him, How can a man be born when he is old? can he enter the second time into his mother's womb, and be born?

Jesus answered, Verily, verily, I say unto thee, Except a man be born of water and of the Spirit, he cannot enter into the kingdom of God.

That which is born of the flesh is flesh, and that which is born of the Spirit is spirit. **John 3:3-6**

INTRODUCTION SELF CONTROL

Self-control is vital in ministry. God tells us in His Word that it is necessary to remain calm. I have had many situations where I could have handled things better. When this is done correctly, our faith grows stronger, and our walk with God grows deeper with Jesus. I am still working on this, and we will be working on this for the remainder of our earthly lives. Self-control does not develop overnight; it takes time to let God and His Holy Spirit work in us. I have learned to let things go—there's no reason to hold grudges or bitterness. It just leads to anger. Allow the Holy Spirit to take control and let Him show and teach you how to handle situations when they arise. People are watching us, and we have to be witnesses to Christ. If we blow up, how can they see Jesus in us? They can't. We need to work out our salvation and work on our character.

How has self-control saved you from a situation that could have been bad, and how can we pray to God for more self-control?

Prayer

'Heavenly Father, give us self-control so we can be a witness to You and not blow up at people when challenging situations arise, we give You the glory, Jesus, for the control You give us to handle things better.'

SELF CONTROL

Young men likewise exhort to be sober-minded. **Titus 2:6**

He that hath no rule over his own spirit is like a city that is broken down, and without walls. **Proverbs 25:28**

He that is slow to anger is better than the mighty, and he that ruleth his spirit than he that taketh a city. **Proverbs 16:32**

Wherefore, my beloved brethren, let every man be swift to hear, slow to speak, slow to wrath.

For the wrath of man worketh not the righteousness of God. **James 1:19-20**

Set a watch, O LORD, before my mouth; keep the door of my lips.

Incline not my heart to any evil thing, to practice wicked works with men that work iniquity: and let me not eat of their dainties. **Psalm 141:3-4**

Wherefore gird up the loins of your mind, be sober, and hope to the end for the grace that is to be brought unto you at the revelation of Jesus Christ. **1 Peter 1:13**

That the aged men be sober, grave, temperate, sound in faith, in charity, in patience. **Titus 2:2**

Death and life are in the power of the tongue: and they that love it shall eat the fruit thereof. **Proverbs 18:21**

He that keepeth his mouth keepeth his life: but he that openeth wide his lips shall have destruction. **Proverbs 13:3**

There is nothing from without a man, that entering into him can defile him: but the things which come out of him, those are they that defile the man. **Mark 7:15**

That ye put off concerning the former conversation the old man, which is corrupt according to the deceitful lusts. Ephesians 4:22

Be not hasty in thy spirit to be angry: for anger resteth in the bosom of fools. **Ecclesiastes 7:9**

A soft answer turneth away wrath: but grievous words stir up anger. **Proverbs 15:1**

Thou hast proved mine heart; thou hast visited me in the night; thou hast tried me, and shalt find nothing; I am purposed that my mouth shall not transgress. **Psalm 17:3**

Whoso keepeth his mouth and his tongue keepeth his soul from troubles. **Proverbs 21:23**

And the tongue is a fire, a world of iniquity: so is the tongue among our members, that it defileth the whole body, and setteth on fire the course of nature; and it is set on fire of hell. **James 3:6**

INTRODUCTION SEEKING GOD

We should seek God in all we do and in every aspect of our lives. Seeking God is a priority. When we seek God, we draw closer to Him (James 4:8 KJV). When we draw closer to God, the more intimate we become with Him. I try to seek God in everything I do. We should try our best to seek Him.

When was a time in your life when you really sought God and became more intimate with the Holy Spirit?

Prayer

'Dear loving Father, show us Your way as we seek You in our life to become more intimate with You.'

SEEKING GOD

But if from thence thou shalt seek the LORD thy God, thou shalt find him, if thou seek him with all thy heart and with all thy soul. **Deuteronomy 4:29**

I love them that love me, and those that seek me early shall find me. **Proverbs 8:17**

Ask, and it shall be given you; seek, and ye shall find; knock, and it shall be opened unto you:

For every one that asketh receiveth; and he that seeketh findeth; and to him that knocketh it shall be opened. **Matthew 7:7-8**

Seek the LORD and his strength, seek his face continually. **1 Chronicles 16:11**

The LORD is good unto them that wait for him, to the soul that seeketh him. **Lamentations 3:25**

Seek ye the LORD while he may be found, call ye upon him while he is near. **Isaiah 55:6**

And ye shall seek me, and find me when ye shall search for me with all your heart. **Jeremiah 29:13**

But without faith it is impossible to please him: for he that cometh

336

to God must believe that he is, and that he is a rewarder of them that diligently seek him. **Hebrews 11:6**

The young lions do lack, and suffer hunger: but they that seek the LORD shall not want any good thing. **Psalm 34:10**

Let all those that seek thee rejoice and be glad in thee: let such as love thy salvation say continually, The LORD be magnified. **Psalm 40:16**

Blessed are they that keep his testimonies, and that seek him with the whole heart. **Psalm 119:2**

And they that know thy name will put their trust in thee: for thou, LORD, hast not forsaken them that seek thee. **Psalm 9:10**

The LORD looked down from heaven upon the children of men, to see if there were any that did understand, and seek God. **Psalm 14:2**

O God, thou art my God; early will I seek thee: my soul thirsteth for thee, my flesh longeth for thee in a dry and thirsty land, where no water is. **Psalm 63:1**

And I will walk at liberty: for I seek thy precepts. **Psalm 119:45**

Seek ye the LORD, all ye meek of the earth, which have wrought his judgment; seek righteousness, seek meekness: it may be ye shall be hid in the day of the LORD's anger. **Zephaniah 2:3**

337

And I say unto you, Ask, and it shall be given you; seek, and ye shall find; knock, and it shall be opened unto you. **Luke 11:9**

Draw nigh to God, and he will draw nigh to you. Cleanse your hands, ye sinners; and purify your hearts, ye double-minded. **James 4:8**

Seek the LORD and his strength: seek his face evermore. **Psalm 105:4**

For thus saith the LORD unto the house of Israel, Seek ye me, and ye shall live. **Amos 5:4**

That they should seek the Lord if haply they might feel after him, and find him, though he is not far from every one of us. **Acts 17:27**

INTRODUCTION SEXUAL SINS

We should flee from any kind of sexual immorality. The Bible says that a man should not lie with another man, nor defile his body. A woman should not lie with another woman, nor defile her body. There are no sins greater than any other sin except blasphemy of the Holy Spirit. If the temptation arises, run from it as far as the east is from the west. The Bible talks about sexual sins a lot. In Genesis 38:8-10, Onan spilled his seed on the ground, and the Lord struck him dead. What he did was wicked in the Lord's sight. America has become modern-day Babylon. This generation is perverse and wicked. We need to pray for America and the nations for the Lord to change hearts. Pray for the nations to turn from their evil and follow God.

How can you turn to God to avoid sexual sins and resist temptation?

Prayer

'Dear Heavenly Father, I pray for America and other nations to avoid any kind of sin, especially sexual sins. In Jesus' name, Amen.'

SEXUAL SINS

Flee fornication. Every sin that a man doeth is without the body; but he that committeth fornication sinneth against his own body.

What? know ye not that your body is the temple of the Holy Ghost which is in you, which ye have of God, and ye are not your own?

For ye are bought with a price: therefore glorify God in your body, and in your spirit, which is God's. **1 Corinthians 6:18-20**

But whoso committeth adultery with a woman lacketh understanding: he that doeth it destroyeth his own soul. **Proverbs 6:32**

Know ye not that the unrighteous shall not inherit the kingdom of God? Be not deceived: neither fornicators, nor idolaters, nor adulterers, nor effeminate, nor abusers of themselves with mankind,

Nor thieves, nor covetous, nor drunkards, nor revilers, nor extortioners, shall inherit the kingdom of God.

And such were some of you: but ye are washed, but ye are sanctified, but ye are justified in the name of the Lord Jesus, and by the Spirit of our God. **1 Corinthians 6:9-11**

Thou shalt not lie with mankind, as with womankind: it is an abomination. **Leviticus 18:22**

For this is the will of God, even your sanctification, that ye should abstain from fornication. **1 Thessalonians 4:3**

Now the works of the flesh are manifest, which are these; Adultery, fornication, uncleanness, lasciviousness. **Galatians 5:19**

And he said, That which cometh out of the man, that defileth the man.

For from within, out of the heart of men, proceed evil thoughts, adulteries, fornications, murders, Thefts, covetousness, wickedness, deceit, lasciviousness, an evil eye, blasphemy, pride, foolishness:

All these evil things come from within and defile the man. **Mark 7:20-23**

And lest, when I come again, my God will humble me among you, and that I shall bewail many which have sinned already, and have not repented of the uncleanness and fornication and lasciviousness which they have committed. **2 Corinthians 12:21**

Even as Sodom and Gomorrah, and the cities about them in like manner, giving themselves over to fornication, and going after strange flesh, are set forth for an example, suffering the vengeance of eternal fire. **Jude 7**

Thou shalt not commit adultery. **Exodus 20:14**

And if a man takes a wife and her mother, it is wickedness: they shall be burnt with fire, both he and they; that there be no wickedness among you. **Leviticus 20:13**

Whosoever putteth away his wife, and marrieth another, committeth adultery: and whosoever marrieth her that is put away from her husband committeth adultery. **Luke 16:18**

I wrote unto you in an epistle not to company with fornicators:

Yet not altogether with the fornicators of this world, or with the covetous, or extortioners, or with idolaters; for then must ye needs go out of the world.

But now I have written unto you not to keep company if any man that is called a brother be a fornicator, or covetous, or an idolator, or a railer, or a drunkard, or an extortioner; with such a one no not to eat. **1 Corinthians 5:9-11**

INTRODUCTION SANCTIFICATION

What is sanctification? Sanctification is the state of growing into divine grace as a result of Christian commitment after conversion to Jesus Christ. It is also set apart for a sacred purpose. Another word for this process is to consecrate: to be from sin, to purify, to impart, or to impute.

The Biblical meaning of sanctification is to set apart for God's special use and purpose; therefore, God's people are said to be sanctified because they are set apart. In Biblical sanctification, a person is separated from evil or common use and dedicated to God. Another word for sanctification is holiness.

Is there a process of sanctification? It can be instant or progressive. Instant means when Jesus comes into our lives and hearts, and sin is removed. However, some of our sanctification is progressive, which means we all have things we need to work on. Some of us have struggles we go through; we are not perfect.

Permanent sanctification is when we go to heaven and are eternally glorified, which means death has no sting, and we are right with God. Sanctification is an ongoing process. The blood of Jesus sanctifies us from all sin; Jesus makes us holy and purifies us. The process of sanctification lasts our entire life. Jesus' blood is the only element that can wash us clean. The Holy Spirit will guide us into all truth.

We must cooperate with God. We cannot become holy without the Lord's work in our lives and ministry. We must do our part to be holy. God sanctifies us through Jesus and through His Word. God sent His Spirit to continually do work in us to be that holy saint.

Sanctification is a process. Anyone who says that they have it all is lying, and the truth is not in them. My sanctification from drugs was instant; however, there are things I still need to work on. I do not proclaim I am perfect—I am not, and I don't pretend to be.

How did Jesus sanctify you from Sin? Are there things you still need to work on?

Prayer

'Dear heavenly Father, thank you for Your sanctifying grace that You have given us to be redeemed from sin. I ask you Father, to help us to become more sanctified with the things we need to work on.'

SANCTIFICATION

But we are bound to give thanks always to God for you, brethren beloved of the Lord because God hath from the beginning chosen you to salvation through sanctification of the Spirit and belief of the truth. **2 Thessalonians 2:13**

To open their eyes, and to turn them from darkness to light, and from the power of Satan unto God, that they may receive forgiveness of sins, and inheritance among them which are sanctified by faith that is in me. **Acts 26:18**

Unto the church of God which is at Corinth, to them that are sanctified in Christ Jesus, called to be saints, with all that in every place call upon the name of Jesus Christ our Lord, both their's and our's. **1 Corinthians 1:2**

And such were some of you: but ye are washed, but ye are sanctified, but ye are justified in the name of the Lord Jesus, and by the Spirit of our God. **1 Corinthians 6:11**

Elect according to the foreknowledge of God the Father, through sanctification of the Spirit, unto obedience and sprinkling of the blood of Jesus Christ: Grace unto you, and peace, be multiplied. **1 Peter 1:2**

And the very God of peace sanctify you wholly, and I pray God your whole spirit and soul and body be preserved blameless unto the coming of our Lord Jesus Christ. **1Thessalonians 5:23**

Sanctify them through thy truth: thy word is truth. **John 17:17**

Being confident of this very thing, that he which hath begun a good work in you will perform it until the day of Jesus Christ. **Philippians 1:6**

That I should be the minister of Jesus Christ to the Gentiles, ministering the gospel of God, that the offering up of the Gentiles might be acceptable, being sanctified by the Holy Ghost. **Romans 15:16**

Therefore, if any man be in Christ, he is a new creature: old things are passed away; behold, all things are become new. **2 Corinthians 5:17**

For this is the will of God, even your sanctification, that ye should abstain from fornication.

Every one of you should know how to possess his vessel in sanctification and honor.

Not in the lust of concupiscence, even as the Gentiles which know not God. **1 Thessalonians 4:3-5**

Knowing this, that our old man is crucified with him, that the body of sin might be destroyed, that henceforth we should not serve sin. **Romans 6:6**

For by one offering, he hath perfected forever them that are sanctified. **Hebrews 10:14**

Wherefore Jesus also, that he might sanctify the people with his own blood, suffered without the gate. **Hebrews 13:12**

And for their sakes, I sanctify myself, that they also might be sanctified through the truth. **John 17:19**

INTRODUCTION STUDY

Studying the Word of God is indeed enlightening. We need to take time with the Lord and study His Word. We draw closer to God when we meditate on the Scriptures day and night. I have ADHD, so reading and comprehension can be challenging for me, but I still make time for the Lord's Word. It is with the Holy Spirit's help that I am sometimes given a scripture exactly fitting what others are going through. It's a gift of wisdom and knowledge, and my son has this gift as well.

There are many distractions in this world that take time away from God, and anything we put before God can become an idol. I am the first to admit that I am guilty of this. My phone, for instance, can be a huge distraction. We can serve false gods and idols without even realizing it. Did you know that if you spend three hours on your phone per day, you will have spent forty-two days on your phone over the entire year? I heard a message on this, did the math, and found it to be correct. That realization hit me like a ton of bricks.

So, I have made some sacrifices to spend as much time as I can with the Lord and to be obedient. The Holy Spirit teaches all things (John 14:26 KJV). We should meditate on His Word day and night.

To let go of distractions and go further in God's Word, we need to prioritize our time and be intentional about our study. When I received my associate's degree in Biblical Studies, I was filled with joy, knowing that hard work had paid off. I often think of ways to immerse myself more in the Word beyond what I am currently studying. My family and I read six chapters per night: three from the Old Testament and three from the New Testament. After each chapter, we discuss it, which usually takes about an hour. We then pray and ask the Lord to help us understand His Word better.

We will never know everything about the Bible, but we can always learn more. God wants us to fully commit to studying His Word.

How can we get into the Word of God more and allow the Holy Spirit to help us understand what we are reading and studying?

Prayer

'Heavenly Father, send Your Holy Spirit to help us to understand Your Word better and to apply the Word to our lives.'

STUDY

All scripture is given by inspiration of God, and is profitable for doctrine, for reproof, for correction, for instruction in righteousness:

That the man of God may be perfect, thoroughly furnished unto all good works. **2 Timothy 3:16-17**

These were more noble than those in Thessalonica, in that they received the word with all readiness of mind, and searched the scriptures daily, whether those things were so. **Acts 17:11**

Thy word have I hid in mine heart, that I might not sin against thee. **Psalm 119:11**

Study to shew thyself approved unto God, a workman that needeth not to be ashamed, rightly dividing the word of truth. **2 Timothy 2:15**

This book of the law shall not depart out of thy mouth, but thou shalt meditate therein day and night, that thou mayest observe to do according to all that is written therein: for then thou shalt make thy way prosperous, and then thou shalt have good success. **Joshua 1:8**

But continue thou in the things which thou hast learned and hast been assured of, knowing of whom thou hast learned them;

And that from a child thou hast known the holy scriptures, which are able to make thee wise unto salvation through faith which is in Christ Jesus. **2 Timothy 3:14-15**

Search the scriptures; for in them ye think ye have eternal life: and they are they which testify of me. **John 5:39**

But he said, Yeah, rather, blessed are they that hear the word of God, and keep it. **Luke 11:28**

Knowing this first, that no prophecy of the scripture is of any private interpretation.

For the prophecy came not in old time by the will of man: but holy men of God spake as they were moved by the Holy Ghost. **2 Peter 1:20-21**

The grass withereth, the flower fadeth: but the word of our God shall stand forever. **Isaiah 40:8**

I am Alpha and Omega, the beginning and the ending, saith the Lord, which is, and which was, and which is to come, the Almighty. **Revelation 1:3**

Then opened he their understanding, that they might understand the scriptures. **Luke 24:45**

Heaven and earth shall pass away, but my words shall not pass away. **Matthew 24:35**

So shall my word be that goeth forth out of my mouth: it shall not return unto me void, but it shall accomplish that which I please, and it shall prosper in the thing whereto I sent it. **Isaiah 55:11**

And the things that thou hast heard of me among many witnesses, the same commit thou to faithful men, who shall be able to teach others also. **2 Timothy 2:2**

The entrance of thy words giveth light; it giveth understanding unto the simple. **Psalm 119:130**

In the beginning was the Word, and the Word was with God, and the Word was God. **John 1:1**

Jesus answered and said unto them, Ye do err, not knowing the scriptures, nor the power of God. **Matthew 22:29**

And Philip ran thither to him, and heard him read the prophet Esaias, and said, Understandest thou what thou readest? **Acts 8:30**

He that believeth on me, as the scripture hath said, out of his belly shall flow rivers of living water. **John 7:38**

Wherefore laying aside all malice, and all guile, and hypocrisies, and envies, and all evil speakings.

As newborn babes, desire the sincere milk of the word, that ye may grow thereby. **1 Peter 2:1-2**

Every word of God is pure: he is a shield unto them that put their trust in him.

Add thou not unto his words, lest he reprove thee, and thou be found a liar. **Proverbs 30:5-6**

Whom shall he teach knowledge? and whom shall he make to understand doctrine? them that are weaned from the milk, and drawn from the breasts.

For precept must be upon precept, precept upon precept; line upon line, line upon line; here a little, and there a little: **Isaiah 28:9-10**

I marvel that ye are so soon removed from him that called you into the grace of Christ unto another gospel:

Which is not another; but there be some that trouble you and would pervert the gospel of Christ.

But though we, or an angel from heaven, preach any other gospel unto you than that which we have preached unto you, let him be accursed. **Galatians 1:6-8**

But his delight is in the law of the LORD; and in his law doth he meditate day and night. **Psalms 1:2**

For I testify unto every man that heareth the words of the prophecy of this book, If any man shall add unto these things, God shall add unto him the plagues that are written in this book:

And if any man shall take away from the words of the book of this prophecy, God shall take away his part out of the book of life, and out of the holy city, and from the things which are written in this book.

He which testifieth these things saith, Surely, I come quickly. Amen. Even so, come, Lord Jesus. **Revelation 22:18-20**

INTRODUCTION TRUST

Do we trust in the Lord for what He will do for us? Can we trust God for everything that comes our way and put our faith in Him? I trust in the Lord forever. The Holy Spirit has put me on a straight and narrow path. We can hold onto the promise that He has given us. We trust Him with all of our hearts. In God, we trust and put our hope in Him, believing that He will work in the supernatural by providing what we need, not necessarily what we want.

I pray that people will be able to trust the Lord for the things they need. I put all of my trust in the Lord; He will sustain us and work through us.

How has trust worked for you to remain in the Lord at all times?

Prayer

'Dear heavenly Father, I pray that we can put our trust in You to work on our behalf. I pray, Father, for those who have lost trust in You that they will overcome this and get it back in Jesus Christ's name. I pray, Amen.'

TRUST

What time I am afraid, I will trust in thee.

In God I will praise his word, in God I have put my trust; I will not fear what flesh can do unto me. **Psalm 56:3-4**

But I have trusted in thy mercy; my heart shall rejoice in thy salvation. **Psalm 13:5**

Thou wilt keep him in perfect peace, whose mind is stayed on thee: because he trusteth in thee.

Trust ye in the LORD forever: for in the LORD JEHOVAH is everlasting strength. **Isaiah 26:3-4**

Blessed is that man that maketh the LORD his trust, and respecteth not the proud, nor such as turn aside to lies. **Psalm 40:4**

He shall not be afraid of evil tidings: his heart is fixed, trusting in the LORD. **Psalm 112:7**

Blessed is the man that trusteth in the LORD, and whose hope the LORD is.

For he shall be as a tree planted by the waters, and that spreadeth out her roots by the river, and shall not see when heat cometh, but her leaf shall be green; and shall not be careful in the year of drought, neither shall cease from yielding fruit. **Jeremiah 17:7-8**

And they that know thy name will put their trust in thee: for thou, LORD, hast not forsaken them that seek thee. **Psalm 9:10**

Some trust in chariots, and some in horses: but we will remember the name of the LORD our God. **Psalm 20:7**

But I trusted in thee, O LORD: I said, Thou art my God. **Psalm 31:14** O LORD of hosts, blessed is the man that trusteth in thee. **Psalm 84:12**

He that trusteth in his own heart is a fool: but whoso walketh wisely, he shall be delivered. **Proverbs 28:26**

He that trusteth in his riches shall fall, but the righteous shall flourish as a branch. **Proverbs 11:28**

Then was the king exceedingly glad for him, and commanded that they should take Daniel up out of the den. So, Daniel was taken up out of the den, and no manner of hurt was found upon him because he believed in his God. **Daniel 6:23**

Trust in the LORD, and do good; so shalt thou dwell in the land, and verily thou shalt be fed. **Psalm 37:3**

The LORD is my strength and my shield; my heart trusted in him, and I am helped: therefore, my heart greatly rejoiceth; and with my song will I praise him. **Psalm 28:7**

INTRODUCTION THANKFULNESS

We have so much to be thankful for: a roof over our heads, clothing, and stability. The main reason to be thankful is for what the Lord has done for us—dying on the cross for us to be forgiven. That, my friend, should be the number one reason why we should be thankful, because without Him going to the cross, we would not be here. I have a thankful heart for everything He has done for me because, in my past life, I did not deserve it.

In 2011, I bought a house for $20,000 on contract, and my mortgage is only $140 a month. My property taxes are $280 per year. At the time I bought my house, I did not realize what the Lord was doing. Exactly 10 years later, the housing market doubled. I am very thankful for what God did for me. I am at a fixed rate, I have no interest in my house, and I was not even following the Lord at the time of purchase. Yet, He still gave me a once-in-a-lifetime deal like that. I am beyond thankful. Nothing I own is mine; it's all God's, and I give Him the glory for blessing me like this. We owe Jesus everything.

Recently, I bought a vehicle. I thought for sure I was going to need a co-signer. I walked into a car dealership with bad credit and walked out with good credit. When the finance department told me, "You have good credit; we will give you a loan," I was like, "Excuse me, can you repeat that?" It was all the Lord's doing. He knew I was going to need a better car for ministry work. The Lord knew exactly what I needed and gave it to me. With my house, He knew the market was going to soar after the pandemic progressed. I am a single father, so money is tight. I have all I need, and I am thankful for what He has blessed me with.

How can we thank the Lord for what He has blessed us with?

Prayer

'Heavenly Father, thank you for the blessings You have given us; it does not have to be money, it can be small things. We are thankful.'

THANKFULNESS

Continue in prayer, and watch in the same with thanksgiving. **Colossians 4:2**

Being enriched in everything to all bountifulness, which causeth through us thanksgiving to God. **2 Corinthians 9:11**

Oh, that men would praise the LORD for his goodness, and for his wonderful works to the children of men!

For he satisfieth the longing soul and filleth the hungry soul with goodness. **Psalm 107:8-9**

As ye have therefore received Christ Jesus the Lord, so walk ye in him:

Rooted and built up in him, and established in the faith, as ye have been taught, abounding therein with thanksgiving. **Colossians 2:6-7**

O give thanks unto the LORD; for he is good; for his mercy endureth forever. **1 Chronicles 16:34**

For every creature of God is good, and nothing to be refused, if it be received with thanksgiving. **1 Timothy 4:4**

Praise ye the LORD. O give thanks unto the LORD; for he is good:

for his mercy endureth forever. **Psalm 106:1**

Oh, that men would praise the LORD for his goodness, and for his wonderful works to the children of men! **Psalm 107:21**

Let the word of Christ dwell in you richly in all wisdom; teaching and admonishing one another in psalms and hymns and spiritual songs, singing with grace in your hearts to the Lord. **Colossians 3:16**

Give thanks unto the LORD, call upon his name, and make known his deeds among the people. **1 Chronicles 16:8**

I will praise thee, O Lord my God, with all my heart: and I will glorify thy name for evermore. **Psalm 86:12**

Let us come before his presence with thanksgiving, and make a joyful noise unto him with psalms. **Psalm 95:2**

INTRODUCTION VICTORY

There is ultimate victory in Christ Jesus. The Apostle Paul tells the church of Corinth that if we are in Jesus, death has no sting (1 Corinthians 15:55-57 KJV). How has the Lord been victorious in your life? I can share with you times when the Lord came through and gave me victory. Once a drug addict, transformed by the power of the Holy Spirit into a man of God, that, my friend, was the very first victory God gave me: a 22-year drug habit gone in a matter of seconds. Christ's victory gave me a testimony to share with the world about the importance of giving our lives to Jesus and letting the Holy Spirit take control. He will give you victory over the sin that we tend to hold on to. If you're having any struggles, Jesus will shine through and give you victory over the desires of the flesh. Satan has no power over you; he is behind us. The victory that was shed on the cross—Christ's blood—gives us victory.

I went on a mission trip to Liberia, Africa, in December 2022. I was there for a week, and the Lord used me to speak life into the nation. I was invited to go on a crusade and preach at conferences. The Holy Spirit was mightily at work. I prepared my testimony and a message for about four months, but God had other plans. On December 9th, 2022, a day when the angels rejoiced and God was pleased with me, I was about to go into the church in Paynesville, a remote village in Liberia. An African lady from the nation was walking through the grounds of the church. She approached me, and the Holy Spirit came upon me and told me to stay and talk to her. God used me mightily; the Holy Spirit told me she was about to commit suicide. I asked her if she was about to do what the Lord told me—that she was going to take her life. She was going through a lot of battles, and she told me yes. I knew I had to stay there and pray for her. Tears were rolling down my face and hers. I was joyful that the Holy Spirit used me like He did. It was for His glory and not my own. If I had not listened to God and gone on the trip, she might have killed herself. We crossed paths in God's time. When God tells us to do something, we better do it. I prayed for her for a long time, while the protocol from the church was waving me to come in as I was late to preach. I told them I had to pray for her. The Holy Spirit used me to give her victory over her struggles. I am now connected with her on social media. The Holy Spirit will use us for the victory of others, not just for ourselves. I am here to pray for others and give words of encouragement. I am not here for myself; I am here to show people God's glory and how He can use us.

The week my mother and I were in Africa was glorious. I gave my testimony of being healed from drugs, and thousands of Africans were touched by hearing my story of how God saved me. I was there to be a light to the nation that has little hope. The joy coming from the Africans was amazing—having so little but giving God all the glory. Their joy in the Lord spoke life into me. I learned so much from them and their culture. The children were glued to me; we played around the church during downtime. On August 13th, 2022, I had a vision of being in an open field reading Bible stories to many African children. They were sitting down, and I had their attention. That vision came to pass. I was sitting down in an open field, and the children came up to me and sat down as I read them Bible stories. I brought children's books and gave them to the daycare there. I fell in love with the children of Africa; they are the future of the nation, and so are the children and youth of other nations throughout the world. We have to pour out our knowledge and wisdom into them. The Holy Spirit used me to prophesy over the children—they are going to be warriors for Christ and the Kingdom. The gospel will live on in the hearts of the children and the youth of the nations.

The area we went to was Paynesville, Liberia. We were in a remote village with a population of about one million. The nation of Liberia has a bit of the United States in it, as the Americans settled it. It was a project of the American Colonization Society, and they spoke English.

The civil wars left their nation in desolation; most of the buildings had not been repaired. The pastor of the church I visited is a mighty man of God—so humble and full of the Holy Spirit. I have learned so much from him. I am joyful to know a man with such knowledge of God's Word. We communicate quite a bit. He has an amazing testimony of how he escaped death during the civil wars in Liberia. He should be dead, but God's grace and plans for him were far greater than Satan's plans. He does so much for their village and nation. I am thankful to have met him.

The nation of Liberia is very poor. I did not know what to expect. It did not hit me until a few days later when I was alone in my hotel room. I thought about their nation and the children, and I wept all night for their people and children. I could not sleep that night; it was disturbing. We have so much to be thankful for here in America. God put me on the mission trip to remind me to be thankful for what I have. I am not rich by any means; I am rich in the Lord. If I had thousands of dollars to give away, you bet I would start something for their children and nation, but I can't. It breaks my heart knowing I can't help. All I can do is pray for their people and their nation. I pray for them daily and for all the nations. Jesus did say the poor will always be among us (Matthew 26:11 KJV). We do have needs right here in America. I want to go back when the time is right and help lead their nation to victory and be an ambassador for Christ right here in America. Our nation is in dire need of the Gospel. God is telling me to stay put for a little while longer. Our greatest gift is love, and our testimony that Jesus saved us. We have a job to do: to lead others to victory. How can you share your faith? It requires us to step out of our comfort zone. When we are running errands in our town and communities, ask people, "Are you going through any

365

struggles? Can I pray for you?" I have just recently started doing this, and it will surprise you how many people will say yes. We can share our testimony and be a witness for Jesus. There is a quote: "The priesthood of all believers"—all are called to share the gospel. It is one of the biggest messages in the Bible. Go out and be a witness; you never know how God is going to use you for His glory.

During the mission trip, I talked to many people after my conference message in the church. I asked over 300 Africans if anyone was struggling with addictions. Half of them raised their hands. The Holy Spirit used me to pray over their people. I kept saying, "Release, release!" I prayed for the entire church that was in attendance. Some were from other nations. They kept saying, "Thank you, Pastor Joshua." I was so welcomed there; they treated me like a king. I am humbled. I went there to serve them, not for them to serve me. I do have the title of an ordained minister/pastor, but I do not hold onto a title. I held onto the foot of the cross, which saved me. On August 12th, 2022, the Holy Spirit came upon me and told me to read 1 Peter 5:3. This was the day I said yes to the mission trip after praying over it. God told me it was okay and that I needed to go. The scripture said in 1 Peter 5:3, "Don't lord it over the people entrusted to you." The Holy Spirit teaches us things through this teaching. I know not to rule over the people that are under my care. We should not lord it over them. If we abuse our power and authority, it shows people that we are prideful. Trust me, I have witnessed people using their power for their gain and glory. The flocks and the congregations are just as important as the leadership. I have learned so much in the last five years. When I first gave my life back to the Lord, I had a mountaintop experience. I sat on the mountain for too long, though. I was on top for a long time, looking down on the earth. I became prideful by judging people, thinking I was better than them. I am not pointing out everyone's faults, and I have many faults of my own. I am still actively involved with the retreat I went on in 2019, and in February 2024, I was invited back into the conference room. I gave a talk on how to grow through studying God's Word, and the Holy Spirit told me to share my mountaintop experience and tell them I learned much more by coming off the top of the mountain and sitting in the valley at the foot of Jesus and learning from Him.

I read *1 Corinthians 13* and told the entire conference room that if we have no love for people, then our study becomes useless and our faith in Christ and study is now in vain. I heard God's voice many times that weekend. The retreat was glorious. We have to love people. After my talk, a few people in the conference room were crying. A man came up to me, and it was his first time going through the retreat. He said, "Joshua, what you were talking about was exactly what I needed to hear." We both started crying. How glorious that was. The Holy Spirit led me to Exodus 33:12-33. The

367

Lord was telling me He was going to give the people at the retreat a favor just like He gave us a favor. He knows us by name; we are His children, and we are favored. It brings me to tears knowing God will do everything that He has promised to do. The Holy Spirit is amazing in how He is leading me because I put God first and trust in Jesus. How can you put your trust in Jesus to lead you down that straight and narrow path? Don't get ahead of God. Stay in the Word, remain faithful, and close to Him. He will show you which path to take. It is like driving to a T-intersection; you can only go left or right. Which way is God's way, and which way will lead us to destruction or failure? Pray and ask God; He will surely tell you which way to go to lead you to victory.

The Holy Spirit has led me all the way to discover my calling: to take as many with me as I can and to be an ambassador for Christ wherever the Holy Spirit leads me. He is in control of my life; He is driving for me. If I never go back to Africa, it's okay. If I never pastor a church, I am okay with that. I am okay with what the Lord has me doing right now: to serve and not to be served (Matthew 20:28 KJV). Discover your calling by praying and fasting. God will show you which way to go (Isaiah 30:19-23 KJV). I know I have a calling in the mission field, but for right now, I have a son to take care of. We have a priority list: God, family, then ministry. If we get this mixed up, we can't go any further in ministry. I know this because I have been down this road. I encourage you to remain in

Jesus and put Him first, then your family, then your ministry. You will spiritually grow. God wants you to put all of your trust in Him to lead you to victory. You're the light to others for salvation. Pray daily for opportunities to arise to share your faith. Jesus will shine brightly through you, my friend. Victory is waiting for people.

How has Jesus given you victory in your life over the struggles we often go through?

Prayer

'Heavenly Father, thank you for giving us victory by going to the cross for us, use us, Father, to help other people gain victory.'

VICTORY

But thanks be to God, which giveth us the victory through our Lord Jesus Christ. **1 Corinthians 15:57**

For whatsoever is born of God overcometh the world: and this is the victory that overcometh the world, even our faith.

Who is he that overcometh the world, but he that believeth that Jesus is the Son of God? **1 John 5:4-5**

Thine, O LORD is the greatness, and the power, and the glory, and the victory, and the majesty: for all that is in the heaven and in the earth is thine; thine is the kingdom, O LORD, and thou art exalted as head above all. **1 Chronicles 29:11**

Now thanks be unto God, which always causeth us to triumph in Christ, and maketh manifest the savor of his knowledge by us in every place. **2 Corinthians 2:14**

Know ye not that they which run in a race run all, but one receiveth the prize? So run, that ye may obtain. **1 Corinthians 9:24**

And the victory that day was turned into mourning unto all the people: for the people heard say that day how the king was grieved for his son. **2 Samuel 19:2**

He arose and smote the Philistines until his hand was weary, and his hand clave unto the sword: and the LORD wrought a great victory that day, and the people returned after him only to spoil. **2 Samuel 23:10**

O sing unto the LORD a new song; for he hath done marvelous things: his right hand, and his holy arm, hath gotten him the victory. **Psalm 98:1**

He will swallow up death in victory, and the Lord GOD will wipe away tears from off all faces; and the rebuke of his people shall he take away from off all the earth: for the LORD hath spoken it. **Isaiah 25:8**

A bruised reed shall he not break, and smoking flax shall he not quench, till he sends forth judgment unto victory. **Matthew 12:20**

The king shall joy in thy strength, O LORD; and in thy salvation how greatly shall he rejoice! **Psalm 21:1**

Be not overcome of evil, but overcome evil with good. **Romans 12:21**

I have written unto you, fathers, because ye have known him that is from the beginning. I have written unto you, young men, because ye are strong, and the word of God abideth in you, and ye have overcome the wicked one. **1 John 2:14**

These shall make war with the Lamb, and the Lamb shall overcome them: for he is Lord of lords and King of kings: and they that are with him are called, and chosen, and faithful. **Revelation 17:14**

And they overcame him by the blood of the Lamb, and by the word of their testimony, and they loved not their lives unto the death. **Revelation 12:11**

Therefore, we are buried with him by baptism into death: like as Christ was raised up from the dead by the glory of the Father, even so, we also should walk in the newness of life. **Romans 6:4**

INTRODUCTION VISIONS AND DREAMS

Are all visions and dreams from God? The answer is no; not all dreams and visions are from God. We have to test the spirits and pray. I have had many dreams since I gave my life back to the Lord. Satan can give us dreams to get us off track and off the path God wants us on.

My first dream that occurred after I gave my life back to the Lord was on February 10, 2020. I had a dream that I was in a building in Iowa that I had only been in a few times. I was walking around in the building, and thousands of people were inside. I was amazed to see so many people there. There was an evangelist whom I had heard before preaching in an auditorium. He was preaching to thousands of people. I was amazed to see so many people listening to the Word of God.

I walked out of the auditorium, and a few moments later, I felt a huge shaking, like something hitting the building or an earthquake. Over half of the building collapsed to the ground. The shaking that had happened was crazy; it was a huge, bloody mess. Hundreds were dead. The ones that were alive were running around in total confusion. I was also confused about what had just happened.

I ran to the auditorium to see if the evangelist and the people inside were okay. It was total destruction. The entire area where they collapsed on them. All of them were dead. The number of people in the auditorium was hard to fathom; there were so many people there. I ran out, and everyone who was still alive was still running around in confusion.

A few moments later, I smelled a foul smell. It was so strong that it led me outside. When I went outside, I walked into a huge war zone that was going on American soil. There was a vast army fighting itself—tanks, bombs, missiles, and bullets were going off. It was Americans vs. Americans. I was just like, "What on earth is going on here?" The missiles and bullets were going right through me. It was pitch dark; you could hardly see anything. The sun and the moon were gone. With all of the ammo and gases that were going off, the sky was lit bright red. There must have been a million people in battle. It was hard to fathom. People were dying right in front of me.

After I had seen all of the war going on, I had seen enough and decided to go back inside the building where I had left and went outside. I was going around inside to see if I could help those who were injured after the building had collapsed. Then, all of a sudden, probably 20 to 30 men dressed in black from head to foot—you could not see their faces—marched in. I assumed they were the military. They had needles like the ones you see in hospitals to draw blood. They had the needles, and it looked like some kind of vaccine in them. They were going around, marching, and injecting everyone who was alive with this needle and vaccine. All of them got injected; they did not have a choice. There were thousands who were forced to take the vaccine. Some of the people who were injected were held on the ground, screaming and kicking. They did not want to take it, but they were forced to. The men with the vaccine marched all around me like they did not see me standing in the middle of all the chaos.

Moments later, my dad, my mom, my son, my brother, and I were standing against a wall. Those people dressed in black marched right past us. I assumed they were the military. After that, I woke up. I asked God what that was all about. That was a wild and crazy dream. I had never had a dream like that before.

A few weeks later, on March 16, 2020, when the lockdowns were starting to take place in America, I was standing at my desk. I grabbed my Bible and opened up to exactly this passage: "Go, my people, enter your rooms and shut the doors behind you; hide yourselves for a little while until his wrath has passed by. See, the Lord is coming out of his dwelling to punish the people of the earth for their sins; the earth will disclose the blood shed on it; the earth will conceal its slain no longer" (Isaiah 26:20-21).

Wow, how crazy was that? I read that passage once and memorized it. Usually, it takes me a little time to memorize Scripture, but not that one. It had a significant meaning to it. Little did I know the entire world would be on restrictions and lockdowns shortly after I had read that. It was a time of stress. Many people here in America were not essential workers or had lost their jobs. About eight months later, a vaccine came out for COVID-19, like what I had seen in my dream in February 2020.

It took me about a year of fasting and praying for God to reveal this dream to me. The entire dream—I was invisible to the enemy. If we hide the word of God in our hearts, we will be safe from the enemy.

Is there a war coming to America if our country does not change? I don't know. America is rebellious and wicked. Most nations in the Old Testament were destroyed once they had rebelled against God and refused to change. We have to pray for America. I have had many dreams of war and famine coming to America for a long time. I chased this dream; I had been consumed with it. God does not want us to follow dreams; He wants us to follow Him. During that time, I was thinking, "Had God shown me a glimpse into what the tribulation will look like?" I don't know, but it was total destruction.

What I do know is that God wants us to repent and turn away. For nearly two years after my dream, I was speaking to people that a war was coming to America, and it could happen—we just don't know when. You have a dream; it's better to give it to God. I am still praying that God gives America grace. We have to change and run from sin. Maybe the reason why I had this dream was to pray for America instead of telling people a war was coming.

During the tribulation, there will be total chaos and destruction. I am praying people will accept Jesus before the rapture takes place. If you're not with God, it's going to be bad. We have a job to do: pray for people to change. My family also has had dreams of a war coming to America. It may happen; I hope not. It's not a coincidence, though, that I saw a vaccine in my dream, chaos, and war.

Look what happened during the peak of COVID-19—riots happened all across this nation, confusion on what to believe, and there was total confusion in my dream. I had witnessed a pandemic in America before it actually happened. I can remember having a prayer group with our church in the last week of February 2020, and our pastor was talking about coronavirus. I was like, "What is that?" I did not share my dream with people until a few months after I had the dream. It just hit me. I saw a lot in the dream before it happened.

Could an earthquake hit Iowa like what happened in my dream four years ago? Jesus does talk about earthquakes in various places (Matthew 24:7 KJV). We have to be prepared at all times, no matter what. Shortly after my dream, God told me to grab as many Bibles as I could and store them in my house. People are going to be seeking answers when times get worse. I have been praying for four years over what God has told me about storing up Bibles. Many will come to Christ after the rapture takes place, and the Bibles and letters I am leaving behind, I am praying people find what they were missing and accept Jesus Christ as their Lord and Savior.

It would not be a bad idea to store up food and water.

In July of 2022, I met a man at a retreat. I got to talking to him; he was going to school for civil engineering, and after the retreat, he decided to take up some pastoral classes. A few weeks later, I had a dream that the man I met at the retreat was sitting on a couch holding his college books and his pastoral books. He was confused, waving them both up and down, saying, "I don't know what to do." I could see the look on his face—total confusion.

I decided to fast and pray for him and the dream. The Lord told me a few days later to go to his job and talk to him, so I did. I told him about the dream I had about him—that he was confused about whether to pursue civil engineering or pastoral classes, waving the books in the air, not knowing what to do, and that he was stressed out. There was utter silence for a few moments. He then told me, "When I pulled into work this afternoon, I was praying to God, asking what I should do. I am confused and stressed out. Then you come here and tell me this."

I told him I would come back and talk to him when he got off work. When I came back, he told me that he could not think when he went back to work after I came in and told him about my dream. If I had come any sooner, he might not have received it.

So, when we get a dream like this, we have to pray and wait upon the Lord for the right time. I counseled him that night, telling him, "The Lord wants you to stay in college for civil engineering; this is your calling right now. Being a pastor could be your calling later on in life. God is using me to keep you on the path that He wants you on." The Holy Spirit used me mightily that night. I went home and gave God the glory for using me to help my friend stay on the right path. I cried out to the Lord in total surrender, amazed at how He used me. He has used me several times like this. It's not me; it's Him.

On July 18, 2022, I had a dream that I was swimming in the middle of the ocean, enjoying some waves. All of a sudden, the waves started to recede and go down. They went all the way down to nothing. I was in ankle-deep water. The entire ocean was nearly gone. I was standing on the bottom of the ocean floor, wondering, "What just happened? Why has the ocean water gone down to almost nothing?"

Moments later, I was swimming in an indoor pool. It was the same as swimming in ocean water. The waves were big at first, just like what the ocean looked like. The waves and the water started to recede and go down. They went down to nothing, just like the ocean did. I was in ankle-deep water. I got out of the pool, climbed onto the diving board, and jumped off, diving into nothing.

I got out of the pool and saw thousands of people standing around me. One of the people started speaking: "Do we want to go the Corinthians way or God's way?" They decided to go the way of the Corinthians and left me as the only one standing on God's word. After that, I woke up. I asked God about the dream and requested an interpretation. God told me the waves and waters represented the people, and the way some of the churches went, following their own way and not God's way.

Look what happened during the peak of COVID-19. The number of some churches went down, and some went down to nothing. This dream resembles what happened during the pandemic when the government had restrictions and told us we could only gather in small numbers. Some listened to that. Could this dream also be a warning of future times, as described in 2 Thessalonians 2:1-3, with an even greater falling away soon to come as written in the Word of God? I don't know. We must keep the faith, which the church was built on— that is, Jesus Christ, the true and firm foundation of the church.

I am praying for some kind of revival. Could another pandemic happen? I wouldn't doubt it. Anything is possible now. The Bible does not describe a worldwide revival to take place, only a greater falling away. It's what the Word of God says. I do believe we are in the last days. Prophecy is unfolding right before our eyes, and some still reject the truth. That's hard to fathom.

What will happen to America? We don't know. We need to stand up for the truth and pray at all times. In *2 Timothy 3*, it says that in the last days, people will be lovers of themselves, covetous, boasters, proud, blasphemous, disobedient to parents, unthankful, and unholy. I do believe we are in the last days. Take a good look around us—look at what is going on. The signs of the times are evident. The day of the Lord is near. The times we live in are evident. I believe the rapture will take place soon. We don't know when, but the return of the Lord is soon. Be prepared at all times, living a holy life pleasing to God.

I want to remind the nations to turn back to God before it is too late. Turn to Jesus, the Holy One of Israel, or suffer the consequences. No one is too far off to receive Jesus. We need to pray for them to turn from their wickedness and turn to God, and pray for the nations and their governments. I do believe a great shaking is soon to come to America to awaken the people. I'm not sure, but I wouldn't doubt it. All that has been going on since the pandemic started, and maybe another pandemic.

On March 11th, 2022, I had a dream that I was in a hotel complex. I was with a group of people; we were standing outside. I had just happened to look up at the sky. It was pitch black. I saw bombs in the air. I was screaming, "Get down! Take cover! We are going to get hit!" They went far off to another land. The bombs did not hit where we were. After that, I found myself in a field out in the middle of nowhere. I walked up to a farmhouse, and there was a weird-looking lady standing in the middle of the field. She was holding a shepherd's cane, and thousands of sheep were running around her. I noticed in the distance there was a sheep pen, and the gate was open. The lady had blue skin and was very ugly, with bright red eyes. She resembled Jezebel, and the sheep resembled God's people. Satan is not hiding anymore, and the Devil is behind the pulpit in some churches, controlling what the church does. Sin cannot be tolerated in our churches, homes, and nations. The pastors who marry same-sex couples are going to suffer consequences unless they repent and turn away from wickedness. What some churches are doing regarding same-sex marriages is an abomination to God and what His Word says we should do. We should love people, but not condone sin in our churches. We need to preach truth and love. I understand we need to love people, but the lady in my dream

382

resembles Satan, controlling some churches. When pastors marry same-sex couples, that is demonic activity. The churches that allow this sin will answer to God. We should let love be our greatest aim, but there is a line we should not cross. The leadership that condones sin will suffer the consequences. Pastors who allow same-sex marriages will answer to God unless they repent and turn away from wickedness.

God is not happy with what is going on in some of His churches. Repent, turn away, and ask for forgiveness. I am praying that some of the churches that allow sin continue to turn away from their wickedness. I am not judging them, but writing this out of pure love. God loves them, and so do I, but He cannot allow this to continue. I was a part of a denomination that supported same-sex marriages. Once my family and I learned of this, we left the church. If you know what is going on and stay with that church, you're just as bad as them. If this continues, the Holy Spirit might bring about a leadership change to put in place those who will obey the Word. America is full of wickedness and perversion. We are not far from a war coming here. Love all people, but do not condone sin in the church. The Bible has not changed and never will. The world has changed, but that does not mean we have to adapt to its customs. I am praying in the mighty, everlasting name of Jesus that the churches that are not in the Word return to their first love and flee from condoning sin. It is not okay to sin. Repent and turn away or suffer the consequences of God's wrath that might sweep this nation and other nations away.

On December 7th, 2022, I was flying to Liberia, Africa, to go on a mission trip. I was listening to music on the airplane. At this time, the plane was over the continent of Africa. I had a vision: I was floating in the sky, 37,000 feet above sea level. The skies were bright blue. All of a sudden, the sky turned blood red. I looked down, and there was the American dollar bill on African soil. I zoomed in on the dollar on the soil. The dollar was turned to the other side, and I saw the Eye of Providence. It was glowing scarlet and white; it was so bright it nearly blinded me. God told me to read Isaiah 13:6 when you awaken from your vision. The Scripture says, "Wail, for the day of the Lord is near." When I read the Scripture, I was struck by how close the day of the Lord is. Could the American dollar change into a one-world currency, and could the United States join forces with another country? There could be many meanings to this vision. Could the United States become a part of a one-world government before the rapture takes place? I don't know. We need to be prepared for anything to happen. We don't know. I don't see this happening until the rapture takes place. Let's not speculate on what is going to happen. We need to share the gospel and bring people to Christ to escape hell.

In March of 2023, I had a dream of swimming in a lake with some friends I used to party with. The water was filthy, like I was swimming in mud. I could see that our bodies were muddy from the water. I started swimming across the lake to the other side and found myself in a pool, washing off the mud from the lake. The pool was crystal blue. I was washing off the mud from the dirty lake. I got out of the pool and was drying off. I saw my friends from afar, still swimming in the dirty water. There was a barrier separating the pool area from the lake, and that barrier was Satan. They were comfortable in the lake. After I saw that, I woke up. The pool represented Jesus, and the blue waters symbolized sanctification. I was being cleansed from my old self, from drugs and alcohol, and the new person emerged after getting out of the pool (2 Corinthians 5:17 KJV). The Holy Spirit was showing the prodigal sons who were close to coming to Jesus. When I woke up from the dream, I knew I was to pray for them, for God to make Himself real to them. If you have a dream about people you know, it is a dream that the Holy Spirit gives us to pray for them. I have dreams about people I know a lot. God has given me the gift of dreaming and asking Him, "Is this You, God, or Satan?" Sometimes people I know just come to my mind; I know that is the Holy Spirit telling me. God will use you right where you are, and be a light for the lost. Many times, I have had dreams that have come true. When you dream, sometimes it's a warning for people; it's a warning for us. Let's be discerning about dreams. This dream was a call to pray for my friends.

On April 14th, 2023, I had another dream. I was standing in the middle of nowhere; the sky was pitch black, and it was completely dark. I could hardly see anything. I happened to look up at the sky, and a comet or an asteroid was falling from the sky. It was so big it was hard to fathom, like the size of a planet. I was standing a long way from whatever that was. It went down slowly, finally hitting Earth. It lit up the entire Earth at the point of impact, scorching the entire Earth. I was standing thousands of miles away, and the fire that came off it scorched me. My skin was red and blistering. The entire Earth was infected by this falling from the sky.

After what had just happened, I decided to walk around the Earth, what was left of it, to witness and proclaim the name of Jesus. I came upon a house and decided to go in. There was a party going on; people were drinking and doing drugs, laughing and carrying on. I noticed their skin was red and blistering. It had been scorched by the huge asteroid I had seen falling from the sky. I talked to them, saying, "This is an act of God, and Jesus wants you to accept Him as your Lord and Savior. He wants a relationship with you." They all started laughing at me and carrying on like nothing had happened, even though their skin was blistering. Some people will still reject the truth and the word of God, no matter what happens. He wants all to come into a relationship with Him, but some will still refuse and reject, no matter what signs they see, even the miracles that they witness.

Could God have shown me a glimpse into the tribulation? I don't know, but it sure seems like it. Most of my dreams have been about war and famine coming to the United States. I can't sit here and tell you this is going to happen. I don't want to put myself out as a false prophet if it doesn't happen. It could happen; I'm not saying it will for sure. But with everything going on, it would not surprise me. Be prepared at all times. It will come like a thief in the night. Do you have enough oil in your lamp? Don't be slumbering. We have to make sure our oil is full and we are full of Jesus and His Holy Spirit. Don't be like the five foolish virgins who did not take any oil with them (Matthew 25:1-13 KJV). We have to be ready because we do not know the time or the hour. If we are not ready for Jesus when judgment comes, the door will be shut. Don't fall asleep.

I am here to share with you. I am fully awake, not slumbering, doing everything I can to share the good news and my testimony of being healed from substance abuse. My oil is overflowing with the anointing of the Holy Spirit. Is your oil overflowing, low, or none at all? I pray that your oil will be full. We do have to stand up for the truth, no matter what the backlash may be. Let's rejoice in Jesus and take as many to heaven with us as we can. To God be the glory forever and ever.

On February 8th, 2024, my mother had a dream that our entire family was all in her house, and bombs were going off all around us. I told her, "I cannot do this anymore. There are souls to save out there and win over to Christ, and I have to take my son with me." She threw her keys to her motorhome at me, saying, "I will see you in heaven." Could all of our dreams come true? A war, a battle zone coming to the United States? It could, and again, I am not saying it will. It could happen. I can see more shaking coming to America. We need to pray for America and the nations for hearts to change, people to change, and return to their first love. We need to put God back here in America. The United States was built on faith in Jesus, but some people in this nation have turned their backs on God. I am praying for revival amongst the nations, not just for America. I do see a greater falling away, but we can still pray. Is a war coming to awaken the Body of Christ? Judgment starts with the body first. God's judgment starts with the church first. We have to remain steadfast in God's word in difficult times. I am here to pray for God's will to be done here in America and the nations. God won't destroy the Earth by flood ever again. He gave us the rainbow as a sign of that, not a sign of Pride. I have seen judgment coming here. God will destroy the Earth by fire. I am here to share with you my love for Jesus. Turn, repent, and turn away from wickedness and escape God's wrath that will come after the rapture during the seven-year tribulation. God is a God of love, anger, fury, and destruction. He is also a God of love and wants people to change, to accept His Son as their Lord and Savior. Which side are we on? Are we on God's side or Satan's side? Where will we be standing on Judgment Day—a righteous judgment from God, or cast into hell? I want to hear the words, "Well done, my faithful servant. You stood by me and did my will." I love Jesus. Don't you also?

Are you a dreamer? Have you had visions? This concludes all my dreams and one vision. Have your dreams and visions been from God or the enemy to get you off track? Have you had end-time dreams, last-day dreams like I have? I pray that God will use you mightily in these last days to proclaim the name of Jesus.

Prayer

'Dear heavenly Father, I want to thank you for giving me the gift of dreaming and being able to discern, is it You or the enemy? I pray, Father, that those who do dream, You will show them it's You or the enemy, and all we have to do is ask You. I pray, Father, that You will use Your people in the last days before the rapture to lead people to Jesus and do Your will and your missions You have us on. In Jesus Christ's name, I pray, Amen.' Glory to God, Hosanna in the highest.

VISIONS AND DREAMS

And it shall come to pass in the last days, saith God, I will pour out of my Spirit upon all flesh: and your sons and your daughters shall prophesy, and your young men shall see visions, and your old men shall dream dreams. **Acts 2:17**

And it shall come to pass afterward, that I will pour out my spirit upon all flesh; and your sons and your daughters shall prophesy, your old men shall dream dreams, your young men shall see visions. **Joel 2:28**

Surely the Lord GOD will do nothing, but he revealeth his secret unto his servants the prophets. **Amos 3:7**

As for these four children, God gave them knowledge and skill in all learning and wisdom: and Daniel had understanding in all visions and dreams. **Daniel 1:17**

And he said, Hear now my words: If there be a prophet among you, I the LORD will make myself known unto him in a vision, and will speak unto him in a dream. **Numbers 12:6**

And his brethren said to him, Shalt thou indeed reign over us? or shalt thou indeed have dominion over us? And they hated him yet the more for his dreams, and for his words. **Genesis 37:8**

Come now, therefore, and let us slay him, and cast him into some pit, and we will say, Some evil beast hath devoured him: and we shall see what will become of his dreams. **Genesis 37:20**

And there was there with us a young man, a Hebrew, servant to the captain of the guard; and we told him, and he interpreted to us our dreams; to each man, according to his dream, he did interpret. **Genesis 41:12**

And Joseph remembered the dreams which he dreamed of them, and said unto them, Ye are spies; to see the nakedness of the land ye are come. **Genesis 42:9**

If there arise among you a prophet or a dreamer of dreams, and giveth thee a sign or a wonder. **Deuteronomy 13:1**

And in the second year of the reign of Nebuchadnezzar Nebuchadnezzar dreamed dreams, wherewith his spirit was troubled, and his sleep brake from him. **Daniel 2:1**

Forasmuch as an excellent spirit, and knowledge, and understanding, interpreting of dreams, and shewing of hard sentences, and dissolving of doubts, were found in the same Daniel, whom the king named Belteshazzar: now let Daniel be called, and he will shew the interpretation. **Daniel 5:12**

And the LORD answered me, and said, Write the vision, and make it plain upon tables, that he may run that readeth it.

For the vision is yet for an appointed time, but at the end, it shall speak, and not lie: though it tarry, wait for it; because it will surely come, it will not tarry. **Habakkuk 2:2-3**

And there was a certain disciple at Damascus, named Ananias; and to him said the Lord in a vision, Ananias. And he said, Behold, I am here, Lord.

And the Lord said unto him, Arise, and go into the street which is called Straight, and enquire in the house of Judas for one called Saul, of Tarsus: for, behold, he prayeth,

And hath seen in a vision a man named Ananias coming in, and putting his hand on him, that he might receive his sight. **Acts 9:10-12**

Then spake the Lord to Paul in the night by a vision, Be not afraid, but speak, and hold not thy peace. **Acts 18:9**

I knew a man in Christ above fourteen years ago, (whether in the body, I cannot tell; or whether out of the body, I cannot tell: God knoweth;) such an one caught up to the third heaven.

And I knew such a man, (whether in the body or out of the body, I cannot tell: God knoweth;)

How that he was caught up into paradise, and heard unspeakable words, which it is not lawful for a man to utter. **2 Corinthians 12:2-4**

In Gibeon, the LORD appeared to Solomon in a dream by night: and God said, Ask what I shall give thee. **1 Kings 3:5**

For the idols have spoken vanity, and the diviners have seen a lie, and have told false dreams; they comfort in vain: therefore they went their way as a flock, they were troubled because there was no shepherd. **Zechariah 10:12**

VICTORY IN JESUS

There is victory in Jesus, the One who was sent into the world to die for our sins. Satan thought he had won, but little did he know the victory had already been won. On July 20, 2019, the Lord redeemed me from my past. I had been set free from drugs and alcohol. I had let the enemy kill, steal, and destroy my life (John 10:10), but Jesus came so we may have life and have it to the fullest.

I went on a Christian retreat, bound and letting the thoughts of the enemy come in, pursue, and consume me. It was Saturday night at 10

PM. I was in the last chapel service at the retreat, sitting alone. I don't know how long I had been sitting there, my eyes closed. When I opened my eyes, I found myself kneeling at the altar. The hand of God came down from heaven and touched me. The Lord spoke to me, saying, "If you truly love me and want to be my servant, follow me. Go home and change your life."

That night, my life turned upside down. Three things happened: I heard God's voice, I listened to Him, and I was finally set free from my shackles of drugs. I was given victory in Jesus, and my sins were washed away (1 John 1:9).

Jesus came to purify us, wash away our sins, and set us apart. How wonderful is that? How can we thank Jesus for coming into this world to forgive us and set us free from our sins?

Prayer

'Heavenly Father, thank you for coming to this world to set us free. Please show us Your perfect love so You can use us to set others free. In Jesus Christ's name, we pray, Amen.'

INTRODUCTION WISDOM

There is victory in Jesus, the One who was sent into the world to die for our sins. Satan thought he had won, but little did he know the victory had already been won. On July 20, 2019, the Lord redeemed me from my past. I had been set free from drugs and alcohol. I had let the enemy kill, steal, and destroy my life (John 10:10), but Jesus came so we may have life and have it to the fullest.

I went on a Christian retreat, bound and letting the thoughts of the enemy come in, pursue, and consume me. It was Saturday night at 10

PM. I was in the last chapel service at the retreat, sitting alone. I don't know how long I had been sitting there, my eyes closed. When I opened my eyes, I found myself kneeling at the altar. The hand of God came down from heaven and touched me. The Lord spoke to me, saying, "If you truly love me and want to be my servant, follow me. Go home and change your life."

That night, my life turned upside down. Three things happened: I heard God's voice, I listened to Him, and I was finally set free from my shackles of drugs. I was given victory in Jesus, and my sins were washed away (1 John 1:9).

Jesus came to purify us, wash away our sins, and set us apart. How wonderful is that? How can we thank Jesus for coming into this world to forgive us and set us free from our sins?

When was a time when you asked the Lord for wisdom and the Holy Spirit came through and gave you far more than what you asked for?

Prayer

'Heavenly Father, please give us the wisdom we need to lead Your people, give us sound wisdom to be able to make good decisions when we need to. Thank you Jesus for the wisdom You give us.'

WISDOM

Who is a wise man and endowed with knowledge among you? let him shew out of a good conversation his works with meekness of wisdom. **James 3:13**

With the ancient is wisdom; and in the length of days understanding. **Job 12:12**

For the LORD giveth wisdom: out of his mouth cometh knowledge and understanding. **Proverbs 2:6**

Wisdom is the principal thing; therefore, get wisdom: and with all thy getting gets understanding. **Proverbs 4:7**

The fear of the LORD is the beginning of wisdom: and the knowledge of the holy is understanding. **Proverbs 9:10**

The fear of the LORD is the beginning of wisdom: and the knowledge of the holy is understanding. **Proverbs 16:16**

He that getteth wisdom loveth his own soul: he that keepeth understanding shall find good. **Proverbs 19:8**

Only by pride cometh contention: but with the well-advised is wisdom. **Proverbs 13:10**

The mouth of the righteous speaketh wisdom, and his tongue talketh of judgment. **Psalm 37:30**

See then that ye walk circumspectly, not as fools, but as wise, Redeeming the time, because the days are evil. **Ephesians 5:15-16**

Walk in wisdom toward them that are without, redeeming the time.

Let your speech be always with grace, seasoned with salt, that ye may know how ye ought to answer every man. **Colossians 4:5-6**

The fear of the LORD is the beginning of knowledge: but fools despise wisdom and instruction. **Proverbs 1:7**

For God giveth to a man that is good in his sight wisdom, and knowledge, and joy: but to the sinner he giveth travail, to gather and to heap up, that he may give to him that is good before God. This also is vanity and vexation of spirit. **Ecclesiastes 2:26**

Happy is the man that findeth wisdom, and the man that getteth understanding. **Proverbs 3:13**

That the God of our Lord Jesus Christ, the Father of glory, may give unto you the spirit of wisdom and revelation in the knowledge of him. **Ephesians 1:17**

INTRODUCTION WORK

Work is not always easy. We should work for the Lord and not for men. My job is challenging at times, but we are working for God. Many times, I have lost my cool, and that, my friend, is not the way to handle things. When we lash out, it only shows people—our coworkers and our loved ones—that when we blow up, we act like the world and not like Christians. Our character is then seen from a worldly view, and we are not the Christians we claim to be. Our behavior becomes a sin. It happens more than we like to admit.

We have to ask for forgiveness, and though it's hard to do, if we don't, God will not bring us any further in our walk with Him. The Holy Spirit will work in you when the challenge comes your way. Just be nice and love them anyway, just as Jesus loves and forgives us.

We are missionaries right where we are. We don't have to go overseas to share the gospel; we can do this right in our own backyard, at our jobs, and with our family and loved ones. Five years ago, when I gave my life back to the Lord, I did not have this kind of wisdom. Not too long ago, when people would say things to me to get a rise out of me, I would just walk away, loving them. Walking away is what the Lord desires of us. It proves to people that we are not of this world; we belong to Christ and His Kingdom.

If I had done this five years ago, I would have been better off.

We are all still learning. It is never too late to start over and work on our attitude toward people. The Holy Spirit will show you how to do that.

How has work been challenging for you, and how did the Holy Spirit help you to overcome this area in your life, to love people unconditionally?

Prayer

'Loving Father teaches us to walk in upright paths so when challenging situations arise, we can use Your strength to overcome any obstacles that might hinder us in showing people Your ultimate love.'

How do we value our work? Do we like our job? The Bible says in *Colossians 3:23*, "Whatever you do, work at it with all your heart, as working for the Lord, not for men." With this Scripture God has given us, we are supposed to work for the Lord.

How do we value our work? Do we look at our job as worship? We should look at it this way: our work could potentially be missionary work. We don't have to literally go to another country to be a missionary; you can be a missionary right at your job. God is seen in us while we work. I fail at this a lot, but we should always be Christ in our jobs, allowing others to see a change in us.

Work can be challenging. There are situations we often get into that could either glorify God or harm our ministry. The job I am in challenges me every day. If we fail, we should ask our coworkers to forgive us when we get upset with them. It harms us when they think, "How are they Christians, yet acting like the world?" In *Colossians 3:2*, the Apostle Paul wrote to the church in Colossae, "Set your mind on things above, not on earthly things." Let the things of this world go, and be respectful to people. Let God work through us and glorify Him through our work, and Christ will be seen.

Let's look at work as worship and let God be glorified through our work.

How do we value our work as worship to Jesus, and how can we change our attitudes about our job?

Prayer

'Lord Father, we thank you for the work You have given us as a tool to be effective witnesses, please allow us to be a vessel to You through our work and when challenging situations arise, we ask You to come in and work through us to be that light and person You have called us to be. In Jesus Christ's name, we pray, Amen.'

WORK

And whatsoever ye do, do it heartily, as to the Lord, and not unto men. **Colossians 3:23**

Let him that stole steal no more: but rather let him labor, working with his hands the thing which is good, that he may have to give to him that needeth. **Ephesians 4:28**

Labor not for the meat which perisheth, but for that meat which endureth unto everlasting life, which the Son of man shall give unto you: for him hath God the Father sealed. **John 6:27**

But let every man prove his own work, and then shall he have rejoicing in himself alone, and not in another.

For every man shall bear his own burden.

Let him that is taught in the word communicate unto him that teacheth in all good things. **Galatians 6:4-6**

And let the beauty of the LORD our God be upon us: and establish thou the work of our hands upon us; yea, the work of our hands establish thou it. **Psalm 90:17**

He that tilleth his land shall be satisfied with bread: but he that followeth vain persons is void of understanding. **Proverbs 12:11**

The hand of the diligent shall bear rule: but the slothful shall be under tribute. **Proverbs 12:24**

In all labour there is profit: but the talk of the lips tendeth only to penury. **Proverbs 14:23**

And God blessed the seventh day, and sanctified it: because that in it he had rested from all his work which God created and made. **Genesis 2:3**

And the LORD God took the man and put him into the garden of Eden to dress it and to keep it. **Genesis 2:15**

For even when we were with you, this we commanded you, that if any would not work, neither should he eat. **2 Thessalonians 3:10**

And whatsoever ye do in word or deed, do all in the name of the Lord Jesus, giving thanks to God and the Father by him. **Colossians 3:17**

I have shewed you all things, how that so laboring ye ought to support the weak, and to remember the words of the Lord Jesus, how he said, It is more blessed to give than to receive. **Acts 20:35**

INTRODUCTION WILL OF GOD

What is God's will for us? I know God's will for me, and that is to lead as many people to the Lord as I can. His will is stated in the Great Commission—that it is God's will for every believer to be a helping hand in preaching the Good News.

Have you asked God what His will is for you? If not, I encourage you to do so. It is God's will for every believer to talk about the Lord, share their testimony, and give to the poor. If we do this, God will bless us.

God also has other specific wills for us. Some will become pastors, evangelists, teachers, prophets, or apostles (Ephesians 4:11-13 KJV). This is the five-fold ministry that is written in God's Word. Some will fill those roles in ministry, but not all are called to that specific field of ministry. If we are not called to the five-fold ministry, God has another will for us—His perfect will. He will show you and tell you.

Do not get discouraged if you are not called into the five-fold ministry. That's just Satan's way of discouraging us. God has a perfect plan for you. I know His will for me, and that is to do mission work. We don't have to go overseas to become missionaries, although I have been overseas to Africa. It was an amazing experience! We have plenty of mission work right here in America. We can be missionaries right in our backyards, at our jobs. We are to seek the Lord for His will for us. He will show you, my friend.

Has the Lord shown His will for you, what He wants you to do?

Prayer

'Dear heavenly Father, I pray for those who are reading this, for those who do not know Your will, for them I pray, loving Father, that You show them Your will, for them to put them on the right path, it's not about me and it never will be. I pray Father for Your Holy Spirit to guide them and lift them up in Jesus Christ's name, I pray, Amen.'

WILL OF GOD

Wherefore be ye not unwise, but understanding what the will of the Lord is. **Ephesians 5:17**

If any man will do his will, he shall know of the doctrine, whether it be of God, or whether I speak of myself. **John 7:17**

For whosoever shall do the will of God, the same is my brother, and my sister, and mother. **Mark 3:35**

For it is better, if the will of God be so, that ye suffer for well doing, than for evil doing. **1 Peter 3:17**

Teach me to do thy will; for thou art my God: thy spirit is good; lead me into the land of uprightness. **Psalm 143:10**

For so is the will of God, that with well doing ye may put to silence the ignorance of foolish men. **1 Peter 2:15**

Thy kingdom come, Thy will be done in earth, as it is in heaven. **Matthew 6:10**

Now we know that God heareth not sinners: but if any man be a worshipper of God, and doeth his will, him he heareth. **John 9:31**

Who gave himself for our sins, that he might deliver us from this present evil world, according to the will of God and our Father.

Galatians 1:4

And the world passeth away, and the lust thereof: but he that doeth the will of God abideth forever. **1 John 2:17**

For as many as are led by the Spirit of God, they are the sons of God. **Romans 8:14**

And he that searcheth the hearts knoweth what is the mind of the Spirit, because he maketh intercession for the saints according to the will of God. **Romans 8:27**

And he was withdrawn from them about a stone's cast, and kneeled down, and prayed,

Saying, Father, if thou be willing, remove this cup from me: nevertheless not my will, but thine, be done. **Luke 22:41-42**

Ye are of God, little children, and have overcome them: because greater is he that is in you than he that is in the world. **1 John 4:4**

INTRODUCTION WORRY

We should not worry about anything. We often do worry, but we should cast our anxieties and fears upon Christ. He will sustain us in times of need.

One instance was when I thought I was going to lose my job during the peak of COVID-19. I became worried because the company I was working for laid off 14 people overnight. Fear settled in—I have a mortgage to pay off, a son to take care of, and bills to pay. I went home after work that day and prayed hard that I would not be laid off. I was not laid off, and I thanked God for this blessing.

The company I was working for had only employed me for four months, yet they laid off people who had been there longer than I. It was all part of God's plan; He gave me mercy. We should not worry, because God always has a plan. When we do worry, it only leaves us stressed. We should not worry about tomorrow, for tomorrow will worry about itself.

Have you worried about things in your life, and how has the Holy Spirit helped you through the stress in life?

Prayer

'Heavenly Father, help us through the difficult times that we go through in life, send Your holy Spirit to comfort us in the stress that comes with life.'

WORRY

Which of you by taking thought can add one cubit unto his stature? **Matthew 6:27**

Fear thou not; for I am with thee: be not dismayed; for I am thy God: I will strengthen thee; yea, I will help thee; yea, I will uphold thee with the right hand of my righteousness. **Isaiah 41:10**

Take therefore no thought for the morrow: for the morrow shall take thought for the things of itself. Sufficient unto the day is the evil thereof. **Matthew 6:34**

In the multitude of my thoughts within me, thy comforts delight my soul. **Psalm 94:19**

Let not your heart be troubled: ye believe in God, believe also in me. **John 14:1**

Heaviness in the heart of man maketh it stoop: but a good word maketh it glad. **Proverbs 12:25**

And he said unto them, Why are ye troubled? and why do thoughts arise in your hearts?

Behold my hands and my feet, that it is I myself: handle me, and see; for a spirit hath not flesh and bones, as ye see me have. **Luke**

24:38-39

Say to them that are of a fearful heart, Be strong, fear not: behold, your God will come with vengeance, even God with a recompense; he will come and save you. **Isaiah 35:4**

In my distress I called upon the LORD, and cried unto my God: he heard my voice out of his temple, and my cry came before him, even into his ears. **Psalm 18:8**

If then God so clothe the grass, which is today in the field, and tomorrow is cast into the oven; how much more will he clothe you, O ye of little faith?

And seek not ye what ye shall eat, or what ye shall drink, neither be ye of doubtful mind.

For all these things do the nations of the world seek after: and your Father knoweth that ye have need of these things. **Luke 12:28-30**

I called upon the LORD in distress: the LORD answered me and set me in a large place.

The LORD is on my side; I will not fear: what can man do unto me? **Psalm 118:5-6**

Therefore, remove sorrow from thy heart, and put away evil from thy flesh: for childhood and youth are vanity. **Ecclesiastes 11:10**

But when they shall lead you, and deliver you up, take no thought beforehand what ye shall speak, neither do ye premeditate: but whatsoever shall be given you in that hour, that speak ye: for it is not ye that speak, but the Holy Ghost. **Mark 13:11**

Cast thy burden upon the LORD, and he shall sustain thee: he shall never suffer the righteous to be moved. **Psalm 55:22**

So that we may boldly say, The Lord is my helper, and I will not fear what man shall do unto me. **Hebrews 13:6**

WE ARE MORE THAN CONQUERORS

Jesus' blood conquered death; by His stripes, we were healed (Isaiah 53:5). Jesus came into this world to conquer death on a cross by giving His life as a ransom for our sins. To be forgiven, we have to be fully surrendered to the Lord, and He will give us rest (Matthew 11:25-29).

I am ADHD. I am always on the go, and sometimes I just need to rest in the Lord, knowing He is God (Psalm 46:10). I struggle with anxiety, and at one point, I tried medication. However, I did not like the side effects, so I stopped taking them. One night, I went to a special service to listen to a guest speaker. He called me to the front and prayed for me. He laid his hands on me, and I went down to the floor, slain in the Spirit. I lay there for almost an hour, feeling such peace, stillness, and calmness that surpassed my understanding.

When I got up, I knew something wonderful had happened—God had healed me of my anxiety. Jesus had conquered years of my anxiety in a matter of an hour, just by resting in Him. We are more than conquerors through Christ Jesus (Romans 8:31-39). Nothing will ever separate us from the love of God, who calls us according to His purpose. There is no condemnation for those who are in Christ Jesus (Romans 8:1). Jesus has set me free from anxiety.

In what ways are we anxious, and how can we overcome this?

Prayer

'Heavenly Father, we come before Your throne, we know we can be overcomers. Please, Father, be with us, we ask You, Lord, to help us overcome the things of this world to know You better. In Jesus Christ's name, we pray, Amen.'

LIBERIA AFRICA MISSIONS TRIP 2022

Here are some of the pictures from my mission trip to Africa. It was a trip and a mission that changed my life forever—such a wonderful journey God put my mother and me on. I will never forget it. I learned so much from God during this time with the Africans; they taught me what it truly means to be content with what we have.

The nation is very poor, but rich in God. The joy they had in the Lord, despite having nothing, surpassed my understanding. I am blessed to have gone and made connections there in Liberia. I pray for them daily and for their nation, asking God to give them mercy. My heart pours out for their people. I am forever humbled to have gone on this trip and to witness the love they have for God.

Have you ever gone on a mission trip? Did it change you inside and out?

Prayer

'Dear Heavenly Father, we come to Your throne of grace. We lift up the nations that struggle with poverty and world hunger. Father, I cry for Your people and for the nations to be strengthened. Here I am, Lord, send me (Isaiah 6:8 KJV). Father, please be with the nations. Send them Your love and food to nourish them. Feed them, clothe them. I humble myself, Father, and walk in humility. The day will come when we all will unite in the New Heaven and New Earth. There shall be no sickness, no disease, no tears, no poverty, no hunger—only rejoicing with You in a city that will be forever. Father, please be with all the missionaries in the world who are spreading Your Word and hope. Protect them from danger and keep the enemy far away from them. In the everlasting mighty name of Jesus Christ, I pray. Amen.'

www.ingramcontent.com/pod-product-compliance
Lightning Source LLC
Chambersburg PA
CBHW071219290326
41931CB00037B/1464